THE FALL OF NEW FRANCE

HOW THE FRENCH LOST A NORTH AMERICAN EMPIRE 1754–1763

Ronald J. Dale

JAMES LORIMER & COMPANY LTD., PUBLISHERS

TORONTO

James Lorimer & Company Ltd. acknowledges the
support of the Department of Canadian Heritage and
the Ontario Arts Council in the development of writing and publishing in Canada.

We acknowledge the support of the Government of
Ontario through the Ontario Media Development
Corporation's Ontario Book Initiative. We acknowledge the support of the Canada Council for the Arts
for our publishing program.

*Title Page: A look inside the Jesuits' church after the
bombardment of Quebec by the English, circa 1761.*

Cover design: Nick Shinn

**National Library of Canada Cataloguing in
Publication**

Dale, Ronald J., 1951-
        The fall of New France : how the French lost
a North American empire / Ronald J. Dale.

Includes bibliographical references and index.
ISBN 1-55028-840-7

        1. Canada—History—Seven Years' War,
1755-1763. I. Title.

FC384.D34 2004   971.01'88   C2004-900473-5

James Lorimer & Company Ltd., Publishers
35 Britain Street
Toronto, Ontario
M5A 1R7
www.lorimer.ca

Distributed in the U.S. by
Casemate
2114 Darby Road, 2nd floor
Havertown, PA
19083

Printed and bound in the People's Republic of China

CONTENTS

THE SEVEN YEARS WAR IN NORTH AMERICA

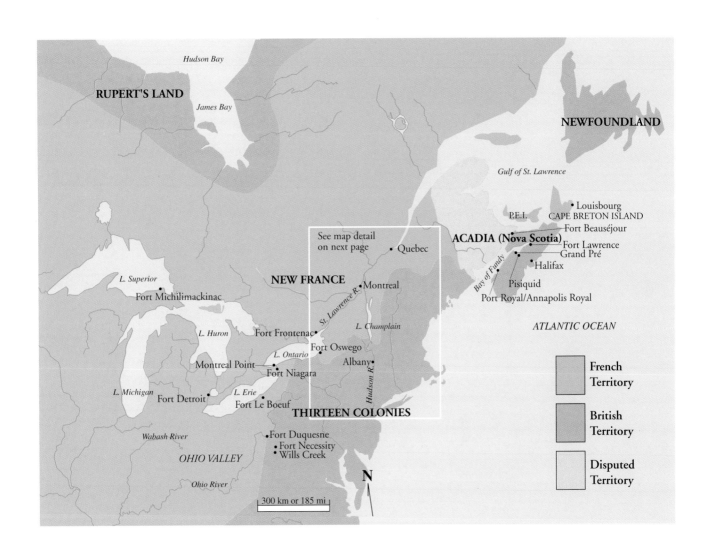

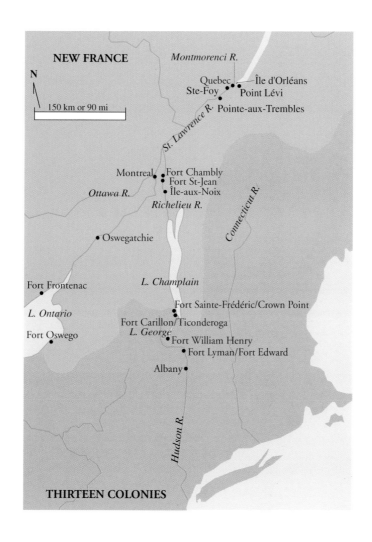

NEW FRANCE

N

150 km or 90 mi

Montmorenci R.

Quebec Île d'Orléans
Ste-Foy Point Lévi
St. Lawrence R. Pointe-aux-Trembles

Montreal Fort Chambly
Fort St-Jean
Ottawa R. Île-aux-Noix
Richelieu R.

Connecticut R.

Oswegatchie

Fort Frontenac

L. Champlain

Fort Sainte-Frédéric/Crown Point

L. Ontario

Fort Carillon/Ticonderoga
L. George
Fort Oswego
Fort William Henry
Fort Lyman/Fort Edward
Albany

Hudson R.

THIRTEEN COLONIES

ACKNOWLEDGEMENTS

The Seven Years War has been of great interest to me for a very long time. I was brought up with the story of the struggle between Wolfe and Montcalm on the Plains of Abraham. A fascination with the frontier, the seed of which was planted in my young mind by the old *Davy Crockett* and *Last of the Mohicans* television series, led me to read the novels of James Fenimore Cooper. In university, I concentrated on Aboriginal and North American military history, with a particular focus on the mid-18th century. Professor David Farrell at the University of Guelph steered me towards a wealth of documentary information on the period and encouraged me to conduct in-depth research on the Six Nations and other Aboriginal peoples in the Seven Years War and the American Revolution. The fact that I have lived and worked close to the scenes of some dramatic Seven Years War events has continued to inspire my interest in the period. Along the way, I have been blessed with many friends who have freely shared information.

The main challenge in preparing this book has been condensing such a complex story into such a short book. Without the guidance of Frank Edwards this would have been even more difficult. The wealth of illustrations in this book is due to the very hard work of Chad Fraser, who was able to track down a treasure trove of both historic and contemporary images. I sincerely thank them for their diligence and professionalism.

I would like to thank my family for encouraging my interest in Canada's past and for having the patience to put up with me while I was researching and writing. Finally, I would like to thank all of those agencies, societies and individuals who struggle to preserve historic sites across Canada and the United States. These wonderful places, where both of our countries were forged, remain tangible links to our fascinating past and are among the most important of legacies that we can leave to our children. It is of the utmost importance that we continue to protect them.

INTRODUCTION
A FEW ACRES OF SNOW

"You know that these two nations are at war for a few acres of snow, and that they are spending for this fine war more than all Canada is worth."
— *Francois Marie Arouet (Voltaire), 1694–1778.*

The French and Indian War in North America was part of a global conflict known as the Seven Years War. This war was the final chapter in the 70-year struggle between England and France for control of the continent. On February 10, 1763, the Treaty of Paris ended the Seven Years War. France surrendered Canada to England and retained only Louisiana and the small islands of St-Pierre and Miquelon from its once great wilderness empire. The war also represented a major turning point in the fortunes of the French inhabitants of Acadia and Canada and of those colonists in Nova Scotia and in the English colonies to the south. The foundations of the bicultural nation of Canada were laid during the war, as were the seeds of the American Revolution, which led to the formation of the United States of America. For Native North Americans, it marked a long period during which they were displaced and dispossessed.

The New World

In the opening years of the 17th century, France, Spain, Holland and England were involved in a long period of colonial expansion. English colonists arrived in Virginia in 1606 and a French colony was established at Quebec in 1608. The two empires clashed briefly in 1614 when the Virginian colonists prevented the French from establishing themselves

A French portrayal of an early Canadien colonist, published in Paris in 1722.

in Maine. More English settled in Massachusetts in 1620 and Maryland in 1632, while the Dutch established New Amsterdam in New York in 1626. European immigrants continued to sail to the New World, the French occupying what are now the Atlantic provinces and Quebec while the English colonized the Atlantic coast.

Samuel de Champlain's own drawing of his first habitation at Quebec in 1608.

Initially, the new arrivals concentrated on carving out homes in the new country, coping with severe weather and scant food supplies and forging alliances with some Native nations while defending the settlements against hostile forces from others. As the colonies became established, however, the Europeans cast their eyes further into the hinterland and a rivalry quickly developed for control of the New World. Further, there were deep religious differences between the predominantly Roman Catholic French and the Protestant English. England and France had been traditional enemies for three centuries. It was inevitable that there would be a clash between the two and that the conflict would continue until one side or the other achieved complete control of the continent.

As the riches of North America were recognized, European powers began to expand their commercial

A modern illustration of a Compagnies franches de la Marine drummer from the era of King William's War.

empires. England, France, Holland and Spain had frequently fought over possession of the rich West Indies, but now the interior of the continent was being exploited for its valuable furs to feed the fashions of Europe. While the French initially explored the Great Lakes region and then the route down the Mississippi River to the Gulf of Mexico, the English thoroughly mapped the country between the Atlantic Ocean and the Allegheny Mountains and began to enter the Ohio Valley. They also began trading out of Hudson Bay, threatening French trade with the Native nations beyond Lake Superior. In 1664, the English annexed the Dutch settlements in what became New York and began to consolidate their holdings along the eastern seaboard. As both French and English courted trade alliances with Native nations, the conflicts among those nations increased, culminating in a massive series of campaigns by the Five Nations of Iroquois in the 1640s to subdue the Huron, Neutral, Erie and other nations.

By the late 17th century, the stage was set for conflict.

King William's War, 1689–1697

In 1688, at the invitation of a powerful parliamentary faction in England, William of Orange and his wife Mary seized the crown, ousting the Catholic King James II. James took refuge in France while the new King William III and Queen Mary strengthened their power base in England. In 1689, the English joined the Grand Alliance of the League of Augsburg and the Netherlands to oppose French King Louis XIV's invasion of the Rhine. The resulting War of the League of Augsburg lasted from 1689 to 1697 and, like all subsequent European wars, had an impact on North America where it was known as King William's War.

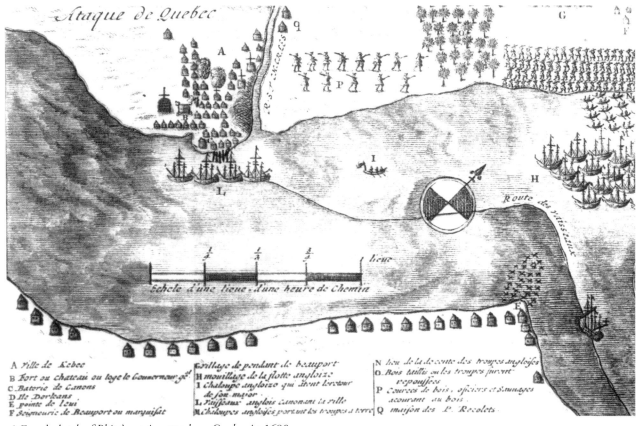

Ataque de Quebec

A *Ville de Kebec*
B *Fort ou chateau ou loge le Gouverneur gal*
C *Baterie de Canons*
D *Ile Dorleans*
E *pointe de l'eau*
F *Seigneurie de Beauport ou marquisat*

Grillage de pendant de beauport
H *mouillage de la flotte angloize*
I *Chaloupe angloize qui étoit lorsctour de son major*
L *Vaisseaux anglois canonani la ville*
M *Chaloupes angloises portont les troupes a terre*

N *lieu de la descente des troupes angloises*
O *Bois taillis ou les troupes furent repoussées*
P *Coureci de bois, officiers et Sauvages accourant au bois*
Q *maison des P. Recolets*

A French sketch of Phips' massive attack on Quebec in 1690.

In 1690, the French from New France and Port Royal, allied with several Native nations, began raiding English frontier settlements in Massachusetts and New York. The English colonists retaliated by counter-raiding French settlements and by launching a grand campaign aimed at the expulsion of the French from America. Sir William Phips, Governor of the Massachusetts colony, raised an army of 400 men in New England and set sail in the spring of 1690 to attack the French settlement of Port Royal, the Acadian capital. Port Royal quickly surrendered to Phips, whose men then proceeded to pillage several Acadian settlements in what is now Nova Scotia and New Brunswick. Phips returned to Boston to plan his next move.

By August, Phips had assembled an army of 2,500 men, loaded them on an array of 32 ships and set out to oust the French from Quebec, an imposing, heavily fortified position on the St. Lawrence River defended by Governor Frontenac and as many as 3,000 men. Phips arrived too late in the season and too poorly supplied to lay siege to Quebec, however, and his inferior army could make no headway against the

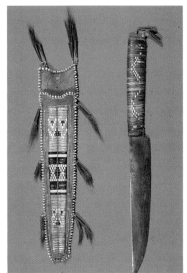

An 18th-century Mohawk knife. Its sheath is decorated with birchbark and porcupine quills.

The Bee*, a replica of a 19th-century schooner, is similar to schooners used in the colonies at the time of the capture of Louisbourg in 1745.*

bastion. Quebec held and Phips retreated. The following year, the French recaptured Acadia.

While small war parties of Native warriors and European adventurers continued frontier raids, no further major actions were launched by either belligerent during the long drawn-out War of the League of Augsburg. The war finally ended with the signing of the Treaty of Ryswick in 1697. The treaty returned the colonies to status quo ante bellum and any small territories gained by either side in America were surrendered. The war did little more than increase the animosity that had been growing between the English and French and their respective Native allies. The seeds of the next French-English conflict in America had been sown.

Queen Anne's War, 1701–1713

In 1701, another European conflict, the War of the Spanish Succession (1701 to 1713), broke out and eventually spread to the New World where it became known as Queen Anne's War, after the new Queen of England, who was crowned in 1702.

Once again, this war was characterized by raids on frontier settlements and by sea-borne attacks by the French and English on each others' maritime settlements and fishing fleets. By this time, the English Royal Navy dominated the North Atlantic. With control of the oceans, the English navy not only prevented supplies from reaching New France from Europe but was able to land invading troops at will on the coasts of Acadia. In 1710 a combined English and colonial army landed at Port Royal and again forced its surrender after a short siege.

The Treaty of Utrecht, signed in 1713, ended the War of the Spanish Succession. Under this treaty, the English gained Newfoundland and part of Nova Scotia. Port Royal, once the Acadian capital, was renamed Annapolis Royal, the capital of the new English province of Nova Scotia. Once again, animosity between the English and French colonists increased as tales of massacres in outlying frontier settlements fed the bitterness between the rivals. Within a generation, war would again embroil the people of New France and the English colonies.

King George's War, 1744–1748

In the years following the Treaty of Utrecht, the population of the English colonies in America continued to increase at a rapid pace. Thousands of people from the British Isles and refugees from Europe immigrated to the New World and its promise of opportunities for people from all classes of society. The new Americans needed a place to live, and canny speculators developed huge tracts of land, often acquired through questionable treaties with the Native populations of the areas. New France grew much more slowly, with settlers confined to the valley of the St. Lawrence River and the scattered settlements of Acadia in present-day New Brunswick, Prince Edward Island and Nova Scotia or to the main urban centres of Louisbourg, Trois-Rivières, Quebec or Montreal. While the British North Americans looked to the vast interior of the continent as a land to be taken from the Native owners for settlement and development, the French looked at it for its economic value as a fur trade empire. As a result, they were more interested in firmly establishing trade and military posts along the Great Lakes and down the Ohio and Mississippi valleys to the Gulf of Mexico. They also recognized the importance of alliances with the Native nations along this route and in the interior of the continent.

In Europe, the Austrian emperor, Charles VI, died in 1740 with no male heir. Maria Theresa, his eldest daughter, took the Austrian throne. Other contestants for the throne took exception to the idea of an empress and war broke out as rivals attempted to oust her. By the spring of 1744, the war had spread across Europe. Once again, England found itself at war with France in this War of the Austrian Succession. The conflict also spread to North America where it was known as "King George's War."

King George's War was characterized by an increase in the guerilla-type warfare that preyed on settlers and small settlements on the frontiers of the English colonies and of New France. While the English maintained a loose alliance with the Iroquois Six Nations, particularly with the Mohawk, the French diplomacy among the Native peoples had been much more

A historically accurate 1925 painting of the English fleet entering Louisbourg harbour to besiege the fortress in 1745.

The Royal Navy besieging the fortress of Louisbourg in 1745. The garrison was forced to surrender on June 17.

successful. The French seemed to welcome close associations with them, living among them and in many cases marrying Native women. They were eager to learn all that the Native peoples could teach them about surviving in the wilderness. Outnumbered by the English, the French regular army soldiers of the Compagnies franches de la Marine and Canadien Militia, accompanying Native war parties, were able to keep the frontiers of the English colonies in a reign of perpetual terror.

The most notable formal campaign of the war in America was the capture of Louisbourg, the formidable French fortress that guarded the mouth of the St. Lawrence River. William Shirley, Governor of Massachusetts and William Pepperell of Maine, with little help from New York or Pennsylvania, embarked an army of colonial soldiers on 100 vessels of various sorts and sailed to Cape Breton Island, arriving near Louisbourg on May 1, 1745. The army of amateurs from New England landed, set up batteries of cannons and began a siege of the French stronghold. Cut off from any relief by the ships of the Royal Navy, the garrison of Louisbourg finally surrendered on June 17, 1745. The French retaliated in 1746, attacking and besieging the English post of Annapolis Royal, but were unable to defeat the English in Nova Scotia. The English continued to control Louisbourg and Annapolis Royal until the end of the war.

The Treaty of Aix-la-Chapelle ended the War of the Austrian Succession in 1748 and once again the diplomats in far off Europe ended the conflict with little regard to North American issues. Louisbourg was returned to France and nothing was done to clarify the status of the interior, still claimed by France and England. The embers of the conflagration that would change North America still smoldered. They would shortly be fanned into a searing flame: the final conflict in the fight for domination of the continent would erupt within six years and would continue until the issue was finally settled.

1

THE SHOT HEARD ROUND THE WORLD — 1754

"The volley fired by a young Virginian in the backwoods of America set the world on fire."
— *Horace Walpole, 1719-1797.*

The ink on the Treaty of Aix-la-Chapelle was barely dry when the French and the English took important steps to consolidate their claims in America. In 1749, the English established Halifax as a major naval base to counter the powerful French fortress of Louisbourg on Cape Breton Island. The French planned major activities in the Ohio Valley to strengthen their defenses and alliances to ensure that the interior of North America, all of the land west of the Appalachian Mountains, would be firmly under French control. This would link the French colony of Louisiana with Canada and confine the English to the Atlantic seaboard.

The acting Governor of New France, the Marquis de la Galissoniére, noted "the absolute necessity of the free and certain communication from Canada to the Mississippi. This chain, once broken, would leave an opening of which the English would doubtless take advantage." He therefore sent Captain Pierre-Joseph Céleron de Blainville on an expedition to bury engraved lead plates at strategic locations, claiming French sovereignty over the entire Ohio and Mississippi valleys and the lands to the west. Increasing numbers of French traders moved into the area while French soldiers began to force English traders to leave the Ohio Valley. The reaction of the English colonies would flare up into the final war between England and France in America.

Only six years after Halifax was founded, the Royal Navy had already established a formidable base there.

The English Colonies

Over the past century, numerous English settlements had been established along the Atlantic coast. The population of these colonies was over one million and rapidly increasing. As more immigrants from Ireland, England and Scotland escaped the poverty and limitations of the old world for the promised land of the new, more land was required for settlement and the land speculators looked to the areas beyond the Appalachian Mountains for future expansion.

The English colonists lived in two completely different styles. Those in the older settlements along the coast lived in well-established towns boasting elegant frame buildings and the finest of furniture imported from England. In contrast, settlers on the frontiers lived in rough, sturdy log cabins, often fortified against potential attacks by Native war parties.

While frontier towns like Albany did include more refined structures, the inhabitants continually worried about another war with the French and the resulting raids by the enemy.

The seats of colonial government were in the coastal towns where the inhabitants gave little thought to the pioneers forging out a precarious existence in the interior of the continent. The English colonies each maintained their own individuality and had difficulties acting in concert during times of crisis. Throughout the previous wars in America it had proved impossible to rally the men of all of the colonies due to intrigues, jealousies and bickering over boundaries between colonies and over leadership during military campaigns. When armies were assembled, they tended to be recruited only for the duration of a single campaign and were poorly trained and equipped. While Virginia's Governor Dinwiddie recognized the threat of the French presence in the

A 20th-century painting of an English fur trader's village near Fort Oswego in 1755–56. English frontier settlements tended to be well protected, while the French preferred to live among their Native allies.

Fort Niagara, essential to maintaining French control of the Great Lakes, was established in 1684.

Ohio Valley in 1754, it was difficult to get the other colonial assemblies to commit to action.

New France

The population of New France at this time was fewer than 70,000 people living in the large towns of Quebec and Montreal or in small villages and farmsteads along the St. Lawrence River. French settlement of the New World had been carefully controlled by the government of New France, which reported directly to the Minister of Marine in Paris, allowing for tighter control of commerce, settlement and defense, a big advantage over the fractious colonial governments of New England. Canadiens lived in the very well-developed towns or in small farmsteads in frame or stone houses surrounded by well-cultivated fields. Westward expansion, settling in the interior of Canada, was not permitted to ensure that a tight reign could be kept on fur trade licenses

and that the hinterland would be reserved for the various First Nations.

The fur trade, an important economic driver for entrepreneurs in New France, was centered on maintaining Native alliances in the Upper Great Lakes and Ohio valleys. Licenses were issued by the government permitting men to venture into the interior to exchange manufactured goods with the Natives for beaver, muskrat, mink and other pelts. Many of these traders, or "coureurs des bois," adopted Native ways and provided an important link between Native nations and the government.

Rival Claims in the Ohio Valley

By 1753, the French realized that they needed additional forts to guard the communications lines between Canada and Louisiana in order to strengthen their control of the interior. They had established Fort Niagara in 1684 as their main stronghold in the Great Lakes region, but now began building smaller forts to link the Great Lakes with the Ohio River, and ultimately with the Mississippi River.

The English recognized these French strategies as a direct threat to their colonies. Orders were issued to the colonial governors to take steps to stop the French from constructing forts on what the English government considered to be English land, "… in case the subjects of any Foreign Prince and State, should presume to make any encroachments on the limits of His Majty's [sic] dominions, or to erect Forts on His Majesty's Land, or comit [sic] any other act of hostility, you are immediately, to represent the injustice of such proceeding, and require them forthwith to desist from any such unlawful undertaking…." The governors were ordered to use force if necessary.

In the meantime, the Six Nations, who claimed ownership of the Ohio Valley by right of conquest, petitioned the English to join them in a war to expel the French. Ohio Seneca chief Tanaghrisson, better known to history as Half-King, had confronted the French at Presqu'ile to demand an explanation as to why they were violating Six Nations sovereignty on the Ohio. Tanaghrisson was not given an adequate answer and was insulted by the French officers. In another petition to the English, he demanded to know why they would not help the Iroquois and associated nations expel the French from the interior of the continent. He reminded the

A fanciful representation of an Iroquois warrior, published in Paris circa 1795.

English that his nation and others had been staunch allies in the previous war. He was not given an answer to this question, although one colony did take action against the perceived French incursions.

Governor Dinwiddie of Virginia, encouraged by wealthy land speculators, recruited a small army to secure the Ohio Valley for his colony by promising the colonial soldiers large tracts of land in the fertile valley. He had appealed to the other colonies for help with his army but only North Carolina responded favourably. A regiment of six companies under Colonel Joshua Fry, with a young Lieutenant-Colonel George Washington as his second-in-command, was ordered to set out for the Ohio country in late March. While Fry continued to recruit in the more densely inhabited areas of the colony, a small company under Captain Trent forged ahead to the forks of the Ohio to begin building a fort. Meanwhile, Washington was ordered to advance with a second party towards the site. Ironically, this was on the same site that the French had previously chosen to build a stronghold. Both sides had independently recognized the strategic position at the forks and both had laid plans to build a post there. The English would arrive there first, but the French reached the site with a larger army and easily assumed control of it.

A young George Washington (right) with frontiersman Christopher Gist in 1753. The pair are depicted travelling to warn the French against encroaching into the Ohio Valley.

The "Assassination" of Jumonville

On April 20, 1754, Washington arrived at Wills Creek, still a long march from the site of the new fort at the forks of the Ohio. His task was to build a passable road from Alexandria through the Wills Creek settlement to the new fort. As he arrived at Wills Creek, Washington received two startling pieces of news. First, a messenger from his old ally, Tanaghrisson, arrived to warn him that a French army was on the move from Le Boeuf. Then another messenger arrived from Captain Trent's company to inform him that a large French force had arrived at the forks of the Ohio, compelling the English to surrender the site to them. The French strengthened the English works and renamed the post Fort Duquesne, in honour of the governor of New France.

Washington's small force could not continue to advance to the forks without major reinforcements. While the English realized that the reports of the French army at the forks were wildly exaggerated, they also realized that their force was too small to face it. Washington retreated to a site known as Great Meadows and set his men to work digging trenches

and throwing up breastworks, dubbing his defensive position "Fort Necessity." The fort was nearing completion by the end of May. Here, he would await the arrival of the remainder of the Virginian army before continuing his advance.

On May 27, Washington learned that a small French force was lying relatively close to his camp. Washington agreed with Tanaghrisson that they should launch a surprise attack on the French. Washington's force of 47 Virginians, with several Seneca warriors under Tanaghrisson, launched a dawn assault on the French camp. The enemy force consisted of 35 men under Ensign Joseph Coulon de Villiers Jumonville. Creeping to within yards of the unsuspecting French, the Virginians' movements were detected by one of the French soldiers, who then fired his musket in the direction of Washington's force. Washington gave a signal and his men returned fire with two devastating volleys of musket balls. The French reeled under the onslaught as Washington's troops reloaded. Jumonville attempted to parley with Washington but the Virginians again fired, cutting the young ensign down. By the time the smoke cleared, 10 French soldiers were dead and most of the others were taken prisoner. One man escaped to travel to Fort Duquesne to report the action to Captain Claude-Pierre Pélaudy de Contrecouer, who had arrived at Fort Duquesne with additional French and Native forces.

A highly inaccurate portrayal of George Washington (mounted) during the Ohio Valley campaign, engraved in 1854 for the centennial of Washington's actions during the Seven Years War.

A contemporary illustration of a Massachusetts Militia soldier. English officers did not think highly of the colonial troops.

Pieces of armour traded by the English to the Native peoples, circa 1780.

Washington returned to Fort Necessity and made plans to advance towards Fort Duquesne, but he did not get far before receiving a report from a scout that a much larger French army was advancing toward him. This army, led by Jumonville's brother, Captain de Villiers, was bent on revenge. Washington hastily retreated to Fort Necessity and set his men to work further strengthening the position. He also sent runners back east to seek reinforcements and bring provisions.

On the morning of July 3, de Villiers' force of 600 French soldiers and 100 Native allies advanced to within musket shot of Washington's rough fort. The two forces sniped at each other at long range throughout the day and while casualties were light, Washington realized that his men were demoralized and his position hopeless. He surrendered to the French in the early evening. After signing the articles of capitulation, he was permitted to take his defeated force back to Virginia.

The surrender agreement is a curious and clever document that refers to the site of Fort Necessity as French territory and the death of Jumonville as an "assassination." De Villiers wanted to present the incident as though it had not been an act of war but rather one of enforcement to repel trespassers from French property. Above all, he did not want the short action to cause a larger conflict between English America and New France. By signing this document, Washington, at least in the eyes of the French, admitted to murdering Jumonville and to trespassing on land belonging to the King of France.

The French used this surrender document to justify the continued strengthening of their position in the Ohio Valley. The import of these events seemed to evade Washington, who wrote enthusiastically about his baptism of fire: "I heard the bullets whistle, and, believe me there is something charming in the sound." The first shots fired at Jumonville's camp in May and the resulting French capture of Fort Necessity in July were the opening actions of a bloody and devastating war that would be fought initially in America, would spread to Europe, and which would ultimately result in the final conquest of Canada by the English.

2

THE COLONIALS TO THE FORE — 1755

"We know our lands are now become [sic] more valuable. The white people think we do not know their value; but we are sensible that the land is everlasting, and the few goods we receive for it are soon worn out and gone."
— *Canassateego, Iroquois chief, 1753*

What had started as a small skirmish in the American wilderness concerned the governments of France and England and, of course, those English colonies with frontiers most affected by French incursions. The French colonists were concerned about English reactions to events and were very aware of the fact that the population of the English colonies was 10 times that of French Canada.

The English Lords of Trade, who advised the governors of the American colonies, recognized their fractious nature. The colonies were continually at odds with each other over boundaries and frontiers. In 1754, they had sent letters to the colonial governors stating the need for a "general Union of Strength and interest" in the colonies. Colonial representatives were ordered to meet at Albany to discuss the coordination of the war effort. At this Albany congress, representatives led by Benjamin Franklin discussed the idea of a united colonial movement. This idea would be revived 20 years later just before the American Revolution.

Meanwhile, General Edward Braddock, a man with 45 years of military

A 60th Royal American Regiment soldier. Troops recruited in America were given a crash course in military training.

service, was chosen by the English government to organize the defense of the colonies and to defeat the French. Orders were sent to the colonies to continue recruiting men to form two new regiments of regular army soldiers and to put 3,000 additional men on alert to be called up for military service when required.

In January 1755, Braddock set sail with 1,400 regular soldiers, some of which were recruited in Ireland, to join the new regiments being assembled in the colonies. He left England with supplies, muskets, cannons and secret orders detailing a grand strategy that would involve a four-pronged attack on the French. The plan was to capture Fort Niagara, Fort Duquesne and the other French posts in the Ohio Valley as well as Fort Frontenac in what would become Kingston, Ontario, and Fort Sainte-Frédéric on Lake Champlain, and to establish English forts to replace the French at these key points. Finally, Braddock was ordered to ensure that the English maintained a strong position at the mouth of the St. Lawrence River. "The last and most material service, that you shall perform, shall be the destroying of the French Fort at Beauséjour, and, by that means, recovering our province of Nova Scotia." At this point there was no plan to completely conquer New France, only to considerably limit the French colony by shutting it out of Nova Scotia and the Ohio Valley.

While Braddock's orders were secret, the fact that he had sailed for America was soon known in France. On learning of Braddock's move, the French ordered General Jean-Armand Dieskau, with six battalions of soldiers totalling more than 3,300 regulars, to reinforce the garrisons of Louisbourg and New France. He sailed in February in the company of the well-trained soldiers of the Languedoc, Guyenne, Bearn, Artois, La Reine and Bourgogne regiments.

Braddock convened a meeting in April with four of the colonial governors and with various civil and military authorities and outlined his plans, ignoring the advice of colonial leaders when warned of the formidability of Native warriors in the backwoods. Braddock showed disdain for the colonial militia

Sir William Johnson, who was well known for developing excellent alliances with the Six Nations.

and belittled the Native fighting style. Natives, he opined, "may indeed be a formidable enemy to you raw American militia, but upon the King's regular and disciplined troops, Sir, it is impossible they should make any impression."

Braddock would lead his regulars against Fort Duquesne. William Shirley was ordered to take the newly created 50th and 51st regiments to Oswego from which he would attack Fort Niagara. William Johnson, who was very effective in developing alliances with the Six Nations, was appointed Indian Superintendent to the Northern Nations and given the rank of major-general. He was ordered to muster an army of Natives and colonial soldiers and to capture Fort Sainte-Frédéric, thus securing the Lake

Annapolis Royal, circa 1753. Recovering Nova Scotia from the French was an English objective in 1755.

The firing mechanism of a flintlock musket.

Champlain corridor. Finally, Braddock informed the gathering that Admiral Boscawen was sailing a Royal Navy fleet to the Gulf of St. Lawrence to prevent supplies from reaching Canada and that a fourth army was to seize Fort Beauséjour to end the French presence in Nova Scotia.

Training the Army

An essential part of Braddock's plan was to recruit colonial soldiers to fill out the ranks of the two regiments brought from Ireland. With land easily obtainable in the colonies and with many opportunities for anyone who had ambition, finding men willing to undergo the rigours of army life would prove a challenge. The previous year, Washington had lamented over the poor quality of the soldiers he had led at Fort Necessity. Braddock would find difficulty attracting anything but the outcasts of society to join the ranks. Colonel Halkett, the commanding officer of the 44th Regiment, had to find 200 additional men in the colonies to bring the regiment up to strength. He called on Daniel McCarty, sheriff of Fairfax County, Virginia for assistance. In the end, the best McCarty could do was to find 200 convicts and unsuccessful tenant farmers who met the basic requirements: that they be at least five feet four inches in height, be able to walk without a limp, have no signs of a hernia or a debilitating disease, and that they had at least two teeth that met. The latter physical requirement was necessary for loading the flintlock musket of the day. Soldiers had to tear the paper cartridges of gunpowder open with their teeth as part of the loading procedure.

Regular army soldiers, recruited in England, Ireland and Scotland, normally received several months of training before being sent on campaign. The soldiers learned military discipline and the daily routine essential to ensure that barracks, uniforms and weapons were carefully maintained. The soldiers practised basic military drill: the positions of attention, at ease, left turn, right turn, slow marching, quick marching, halting and wheeling. At a more advanced level, they learned how to march in a long column and how, on command, to quickly swing into a battle line. They practised how to do a myriad of drills which were so important on a field of battle where the action was normally won by the most disciplined and best-trained troops. The soldiers also practised musket and bayonet drills, repeating the steps over and over again until the movements became second nature. They were expected to perform the moves perfectly, without thinking, in the confusion and terror of battle.

The new recruits in America would have to be given a crash course in military training. They had days, not months, to be transformed from farmers or idlers into soldiers. The intricacies of foot drills and battlefield maneouvres were skipped over and the sergeants concentrated on teaching the

Re-enactors forming a firing line at Fort Niagara. Colonial recruits of the English army were expected to perform precision drills in the heat of battle.

new men to obey orders and to effi-
ciently load and fire their muskets.

The English firearm of the time
was a flintlock musket with a long,
smooth-bored barrel. To load the musket, the soldier reached into his
cartridge box and drew out a cartridge,
which was a tube of paper filled with
gunpowder and containing a lead
musket ball the size of cherry. The soldier bit off the end of the cartridge
and poured a small priming charge of
gunpowder into the flintlock's flash
pan. The rest of the powder was
poured down the musket barrel and
then the musket ball, still wrapped in
the paper tube, was rammed down the
musket barrel with a steel ramrod. The
musket was then brought up to the
shoulder, cocked and fired. The
weapons were slow to load, with well-
trained troops able to fire three and
sometimes four shots per minute.
Muskets frequently misfired, working
indifferently when dirty or damp. Soldiers were not taught at
that time to shoot at targets but simply to learn the steps of

A modern representation of an English 41st Foot Private.

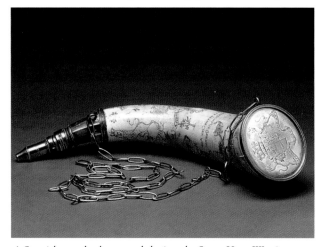

A Scottish powder horn used during the Seven Years War in North America.

loading and firing, pointing the
weapon towards the enemy. The musket of the day was terribly inaccurate
and even under ideal conditions, and
in the hands of a well-trained muske-
teer, could only be considered accurate
at about 75 metres.

As a result, the most effective way
of using muskets on a typical
European battlefield was to mass the
men together and have them fire all at
once, on command. The idea was to
break down enemy discipline and cre-
ate confusion through firing measured
volleys of musketry and artillery fire
and then, at the right point in time,
when the enemy's confidence appeared
shaky, to launch a bayonet charge at
them, hopefully routing their forma-
tions. Troops were trained not only to
attack with their bayonets, marching
slowly towards their targets as if on
parade to maintain formation, but also
to use their bayonets effectively to pro-
tect them against attack. These tactics had worked very well
for the English at the Battle of Culloden in Scotland in 1746,
when the fierce highland warriors of Bonny Prince Charley
had been destroyed on English bayonets wielded by well-
trained soldiers in formation. Undoubtedly, Braddock knew
that English soldiers were definitely a match for the French.
This had been proven on many a European battlefield. He
surely felt that Native warriors, armed with muskets, toma-
hawks and spears, would be no more formidable than the
Scottish highlanders so easily defeated at Culloden.

French Soldiers

The regular soldiers who had been shipped from France were
on an equal footing with the English regulars who had
accompanied Braddock. Each regiment had a backbone of
veterans who had fought on many European battlefields, aug-
mented by well-trained, well-disciplined recruits who were

expected to march in step to the chosen location, move flawlessly while in battle, load and fire their muskets on command, and launch bayonet charges, again delivered as though on parade, advancing steadily toward the enemy while keeping pace to the regimental drums beating the charge.

New France also expected each male inhabitant between the ages of 16 and 60 to enrol in the militia. These men were given rudimentary training by experienced officers but they also received training in the guerilla-type warfare favoured by Native warriors. The French militiamen were not much better trained than their counterparts in the English American colonies but always fought alongside the Compagnies franches de la Marine, a force of colonial regulars for which the English had no counterpart early in the war.

The Compagnies franches de la Marine were regular colonial soldiers under the command of the French Ministry of Marine, represented by the governor of New France. The common soldiers were recruited in France, where they received basic training and were led by Canadian-born officers familiar with the country, the climate and, most importantly, their Native allies. Small independent detachments of these soldiers garrisoned the interior posts as well as the main forts of New France and were skilled not only at European-style warfare but in the guerilla-type tactics that marked warfare in the wilds of America.

A modern representation of the French Regiment de Bearn, one of the regiments that sailed with Dieskau in 1755 to defend New France.

Native Allies

The First Nations peoples of eastern North America came from a society in which men were expected to be able hunters and effective warriors. In Iroquoian and Algonkian societies, women performed most of the tasks related to agriculture and the gathering of other food while men provided for their families through fishing and hunting. Boys learned to use spears and bows, weapons of the hunt as well as of war. Accompanying their fathers and uncles on hunting and fishing expeditions, they learned how to live off the land, how to stalk game to get close enough to use a spear or bow and how to track animals. They also learned how to ambush game, as well as many other skills equally applicable in the hunt or in warfare.

For hundreds of years Native nations were frequently at war with each other. Villages had to continually keep a close watch on potential enemies to prevent surprise raids. Often, it was considered that the best defense was to attack the enemy in a pre-emptive strike. In most nations, the most successful warriors were also the most successful hunters and were greatly revered by their communities. In the winter, when families gathered around the fire to hear stories, tales of the great deeds of the warriors and hunters made an impression on the youth but also passed on many lessons to eager young boys. By the time the boys reached adulthood, they were incredibly well-trained in the guerilla-style warfare that proved so successful in the forests of America.

A 17th-century illustration of Algonkian Indians. Algonkian boys learned to hunt and trap at a young age, making them highly effective backwoods warriors.

Braddock's Defeat

By May 1755, General Braddock set out from Virginia with his army of 2,200 regulars and colonials to drive the French from the Ohio Valley. Braddock expected to arrive at Fort Duquesne and either fight the French in battle on open plains in front of the fort or lay siege to the fort, forcing its eventual surrender. His army brought with it enough supplies to maintain such a siege and to garrison the fort once captured. Since each man required a pound of meat and a pound of bread for rations each day, Braddock's army included numerous wagons filled with barrels of flour and hard biscuits, as well as salt for preserving the beef cattle, which were driven live in the wake of the army. The army moved at a snail's pace on their 200-kilometre march towards Fort Duquesne, moving through the wilderness while cutting a wagon road as they proceeded. Soldiers, wagoners, axemen, dozens of beef cattle prodded on by herdsmen, traders, wives, children and camp followers crept slowly into the interior towards the confluence of the Allegheny, Monogahela and Ohio rivers.

By July 6, the vanguard of the army had finally reached the Monogahela River, camping 10 kilometres south of Fort Duquesne. Braddock waited for the bulk of the army to arrive before advancing towards the French position on July 9, fording the Monogahela for the final thrust. The English army was spread out, with Braddock himself commanding the advance and Colonel Dunbar's regiment bringing up the rear. While the vanguard was protected by scouts who scoured the woods to the front and on the flanks, the difficult terrain prevented them from discovering that the French had set a trap for them.

Native warriors who had allied themselves with the French monitored the approach of Braddock's army every step of the way from Virginia. French officers at Fort Duquesne debated potential steps to meet the advancing foe. The garrison of the fort was small and they knew that if they locked themselves up inside to defend it, they would eventually be defeated. On July 9, with the vanguard of Braddock's force only a short distance away, the French and Native warriors decided to ambush the English force.

Under the leadership of Lienard de Beaujeu, 105 men of the Campagnies franches de la Marine, 146 Canadian militiamen and 600 Native men ambushed Braddock's vanguard, firing from the thick forest and cutting swaths through the packed ranks of the redcoats. As more English troops rushed to the scene and officers tried to keep them tightly packed in ranks, firing volleys into the trees, the Native and French soldiers continued to fire from the protection of the forest. Panic set in and with Braddock severely wounded and casualties mounting,

The Fall of Braddock. *Braddock's men were unable to defend against the backwoods tactics employed by the French and their Native allies.*

A French sundial used for navigation in the wilds of North America.

Howard Pyle's romanticized portrayal of Braddock's burial.

the soldiers fled back towards the main body of English troops. This caused pandemonium on the narrow path and the retreat became a rout. The army became a rabble as they raced back the way they had come, leaving 500 dead on the field. As many as 500 more had been wounded or captured. Casualties included non-combatant wives, children and camp followers. The ambush was a major victory for the smaller French and Native force. Eight French soldiers and 15 Native warriors had been killed while four French and 12 Natives had been wounded.

Lake George

On Lake George, similar tactics by the French would result in a similar defeat of regular soldiers in a backwoods engagement. By September, William Johnson had assembled an army of 3,000 colonial soldiers for the planned advance on the French Fort Sainte-Frédéric on Lake Champlain. He established a base camp on Lac Sacrement, which he renamed Lake George. Here, he was joined by Theyanoguin, or King Hendrick, and more than 200 Mohawk warriors. Johnson built Fort Lyman (later named Fort Edward) at one end of the portage route to the Hudson River and fortified his camp at the other end on Lake George.

French General Dieskau's initial intention was to attack the British fort at Oswego where the Onondaga (or Oswego) River enters Lake Ontario. But along with other spoils of war left among the ruins of Braddock's army had been Braddock's order book and other papers in which the details of Johnson's campaign had been fully outlined. Dieskau changed his plans and marched his army of 1,500 regulars and militia to Lake Champlain. He was accompanied by several hundred warriors, primarily Caughnawaga and Abenaki. On reaching Fort Sainte-Frédéric, Dieskau decided to bypass Johnson's camp to attack the weaker Fort Lyman and thereby cut off Johnson's communication route with Albany. The Native allies with him refused to attack a fort defended by cannons and Dieskau was forced to change his plans, deciding instead to advance on Johnson's camp.

Johnson's scouts warned him of the French advance and on the morning of September 8 he sent out a force of 1,000 men to watch for the French. This force was ambushed by Caughnawaga warriors and French soldiers, and while dozens were cut down in the first volley, fired at close quarters, the colonial soldiers and Natives did not stand in close ranks to

Portrait of Sa Ga Yeath Qua Pieth Tow or Brant, painted in 1710. Brant was one of the "Four American Kings" who visited Queen Anne in London during that year.

face the French fire, but simply moved into the forest and retreated back to Johnson's camp. This short action, during which the venerable Theyanoguin was killed, became known as the "Bloody Morning Scout."

Dieskau's force, encouraged by the quick retreat of the enemy, confidently marched to Johnson's camp. Dieskau ordered a charge but the Canadien militia and Natives refused to attack across a clearing against a defensive position, choosing instead to snipe from the trees at the camp. Dieskau formed up his regulars and advanced towards the camp only to be met by devastating cannon fire. Dieskau was left on the field, wounded, as his army retreated back towards Fort Sainte-Frédéric.

Johnson felt that his own army had been too roughly handled to proceed with plans to capture Fort Sainte-Frédéric. This battle was regarded by the English as a victory, partially offsetting the damage done by Braddock's fiasco two months earlier.

Lake Ontario

Elsewhere, William Shirley was busy organizing his part of the grand strategy, the capture of Fort Niagara. After arranging supplies, and constructing batteaux (large flat-bottomed boats) and wagons, Shirley marched to Oswego, arriving at the rundown fort in August. He repaired the old fort, built two new redoubts nearby and constructed additional batteaux to carry his army to Niagara. Then he awaited the arrival of an army of New York colonial soldiers and Six Nations warriors who were supposed to join him. He soon learned of Braddock's defeat and realized that the position of commander-

A 17th-century illustration of Abenaki Indians. The Abenaki were crucial allies to the French during the Lake George campaign.

in-chief of the English army in America had now fallen on his shoulders. With insufficient men and supplies, the knowledge of Braddock's defeat, and with autumn approaching and storms on Lake Ontario threatening any boat action, Shirley cancelled the planned campaign on Lake Ontario. Leaving a garrison at the new forts at Oswego, he marched back towards Albany with the bulk of his small army.

The Expulsion of the Acadians

While events were unfolding in the interior of the continent, a more controversial campaign was unfolding in Acadia that resulted in actions which, although considered to be very humane at the time, are seen as atrocities in modern mythology — the expulsion of the Acadians.

By the 1713 Treaty of Utrecht, negotiated following the War of the Austrian Succession, Acadia was turned over to Britain and renamed Nova Scotia. The French retained Île Royale (Cape Breton Island) and Île St-Jean (Prince Edward Island) while the area now known as New Brunswick was claimed by both nations. While it was common at that time to expel enemy settlers from conquered territory, the English decided to permit the Acadians to remain in the ceded territories, with the intention of turning them into valuable, loyal citizens of this new English colony. Those who chose to remain were now subjects of England and, as such, the English demanded that they swear an oath of allegiance to the crown. In turn they would be permitted to practise their language and the Roman Catholic religion. The Acadians agreed only to swear a conditional oath, declaring that in any future conflict between England and France, they would remain

The Acadians awaiting deportation at Grand Pré. This dramatic portrayal was published in London in 1850.

neutral but they would not bear arms against their former countrymen.

Following the accession of George II on the death of George I in 1727, the Acadians were again asked to swear allegiance, something required of all English subjects. The Acadians balked at giving their unconditional oaths, which would have made them liable for military service. Finally, in 1729, the Acadian men agreed to a conditional oath, once more stating that they would not bear arms but would otherwise be loyal subjects. This was accepted by the governor of Nova Scotia.

During King George's War, when possession of Nova Scotia was severely challenged prior to the capture of Louisbourg, many Acadians ignored their oaths of loyalty,

perhaps believing that the French would triumph. Some supplied the French garrisons during the conflict and many aided French and Mi'kmaq war parties in their efforts against the English. At the end of that war, the English again considered the expulsion of the rapidly growing Acadian population, but chose

A modern illustration of an Acadian militiaman.

instead to insist another time on an unconditional oath. In 1749 Colonel Edward Cornwallis, the governor of Nova Scotia, called together Acadian delegates from the main settlements of Nova Scotia and again demanded that they swear an unconditional oath of allegiance. Once more the delegates refused, explaining that they would be in danger of a warlike reaction by the Mi'kmaq Nation, who were firm allies of France, if their oath included the requirement to bear arms in war. Cornwallis was told that "if your Excellency is not disposed to grant us what we take the Liberty of asking, we are resolved, every one of us, to leave the country." Cornwallis took no action at that time and many Acadians continued to eke out a livelihood in the occupied territories while many others, fearing the threat of expulsion, gathered their possessions and took refuge in areas firmly controlled by the French in present-day Prince Edward Island, New Brunswick and Cape Breton Island.

In 1749, there were fewer than 200 English inhabitants and several thousand French Catholic Acadians in Nova Scotia. The Acadians primarily occupied farms in the flood plains of the Bay of Fundy where they had built dykes to reclaim rich alluvial soil from the sea. They also spread along the river valleys up and down the coast. The largest concentrated settlements were at the mouth of the Gaspereau River and at

A Mi'kmaq warrior in traditional dress.

Beaubasin. The English had garrisons at Annapolis Royal and at Halifax but controlled little territory beyond these posts. They earnestly began to recruit willing Protestant settlers to fill the province, planning to eventually outnumber and assimilate the Acadians. This proved unsuccessful, however. In 1749, 2,000 English colonists were brought in to settle the newly established strongpoint of Halifax and various settlers, including Germans, were shipped there to begin farming other areas. Most stayed close to the town, fearing the threat of Mi'kmaq warriors who occasionally ambushed isolated work parties from the Halifax or Annapolis garrisons. Eventually, in 1753, a number of German and Swiss settlers were convinced to move elsewhere and the town of Lunenburg was founded.

At this time there was still confusion over the boundaries between English and French possessions in the Atlantic colonies. While England unquestionably held Nova Scotia, and the French controlled Cape Breton and Prince Edward Island, both claimed what is now the province of New Brunswick. To make matters more tense, both sides sought control over the Chignecto Peninsula joining Nova Scotia with the mainland. The English built Fort Lawrence at one end, in modern day Truro, while the French began staking out land for their own fort, Beauséjour, in present-day Amherst. To keep the land between the forts open, the

A View of Fort Cumberland (Beauséjour) in Nova Scotia, *by Captain John Hamilton, an English officer, in 1755.*

Annapolis Royal, Nova Scotia, in 1781. The Acadian population finds its roots in disbanded French soldiers who settled here in the early 17th century.

wrestle a living from the soil of what is now Nova Scotia. Typically, large extended families lived in small frame houses surrounded by a few outbuildings housing small numbers of pigs, sheep and cattle. Their diet consisted of the wheat raised in the reclaimed fields, fish from the rivers or ocean and meat from their livestock.

The Daigle family was typical of many in the settlement. The patriarch of the family, Olivier, came from France, settled in Port Royal in 1663 and married Marie, a woman born in Acadia. Olivier and Marie had nine children, most of whom moved away to Pisiquid, Grand Pré, St. Charles de Mines and Louisbourg. Because families in these small settlements were often closely interrelated, young men tended to marry outside of their own communities. Therefore, most Acadians had relatives in every village of the land. Olivier Daigle's son Bernard, of Pisiquid,

French and their Mi'kmaq allies began a short campaign to drive the Acadian farmers from the area and they succeeded in doing so, destroying isolated farms and small settlements. By the end of 1750, few Acadian families were left in the Beaubasin area close to Fort Lawrence. Many had resettled closer to Beauséjour.

The Acadians

Disbanded soldiers and adventurers from France began settling the area around Port Royal in the early 17th century, creating arable land through the laborious process of building dikes to reclaim the salt marshes of the Annapolis valley. As populations grew, younger people went farther from Port Royal to establish their own farms. A settlement was started at Grand Pré in 1680 and other Acadians spread into the Chignecto Peninsula in the following years, founding Pisiquid, Cobequid and other towns in the Minas Basin. The families tended to be large and the farmers worked hard to

An Acadian farmhouse interior.

and his wife Marie Claire raised 10 children who, in turn, moved to various settlements in Acadia. By 1755, there were a few hundred closely related Daigles in every Parish of the Atlantic colonies, including Prince Edward Island and Cape Breton Island.

Most Acadians were completely oblivious to the political manoeuvrings that led to the loss of their farms and possessions. Like many people caught up in the tragedy of war, few would have thought beyond eking out a precarious living from the soil or the sea and simply wanted to be left alone. While English rule was tolerable, allowing them to continue to live as they had lived, they were morally opposed to swearing an oath that might force them in time of war to fight against fellow Frenchmen. Besides, the Acadian farmers lived in continual fear of the reaction of the loyal Mi'kmaq if the Acadians appeared to be too friendly with the English. Little did they know how devastating their decision would be as war again erupted on the frontiers.

The Capture of Beauséjour

In 1754, with war looming on the horizon, Colonel Charles Lawrence became governor of Nova Scotia. Lawrence recognized the danger to his garrisons of Annapolis and Fort Lawrence, particularly if the Acadians actively helped the French. He was particularly concerned by the steady exodus of Acadians to the French-controlled territory beyond Fort Beauséjour. He felt that in wartime, many of the men of these families could become very effective irregular soldiers who knew the territory around the English forts very well.

Plans were laid for the capture of Beauséjour, and Lawrence issued orders to

Colonel Robert Monckton, who captured Fort Beauséjour in 1755.

his officers to inform the Acadians that "their Happiness and future welfare depends very much on their present behaviour, & that they may be assured, if any Inhabitant either old or Young should offer to go to Beauséjour, or to take arms or induce others to commit any Act of Hostility upon the English … they will be treated as Rebels, their Estates and Families undergo immediate Military Execution…." When war did come to Nova Scotia, many Acadians ignored Lawrence's threat.

On June 3, 1755, the English moved on the French, sailing up the Bay of Fundy to land near Beauséjour. This army of 2,000 men under Colonel Robert Monckton laid siege to the French fort, which was defended by its garrison of 150 men of the Campagnies franches de la Marine, 12 artillerymen and a few hundred Acadians all under the command of Captain Berger. On

An Acadian spinning wheel.

June 16, a massive mortar shell from Monckton's cannon batteries exploded in one of the fort buildings that was supposed to be bomb-proof. The French, now realizing the hopelessness of their position, surrendered the fort. On the following day, Fort Gaspereau, the other French post in the area, also surrendered to the English.

With Nova Scotia secure from the mainland side, Governor Lawrence continued to worry about both the French fort at Louisbourg and the reaction of the Acadians when the war became more widespread. The war had yet to be officially "declared" by England and France. Once again, the governor asked Acadian leaders to swear allegiance. He wrote to the Lords of Trade that he was "determined to bring the Inhabitants to a compliance, or rid the province of such perfidious subjects." Once again, delegates from the Acadian communities were called to Halifax and ordered to have their people swear unconditional allegiance to King George or face expulsion, and once again the Acadians refused to do so.

Lawrence and his advisors agreed to carry through with their threat. They had noted that some Acadians had indeed taken up arms at Beauséjour, that they continued to supply French bases on Prince Edward Island and Louisbourg with food and firewood and that they were no longer willingly supplying the English bases. The Acadians would not swear an oath as English subjects, and could not be simply deported to the French-controlled areas in New Brunswick for fear that this would increase the number of enemy soldiers there. The die was cast. Lawrence wrote that "after mature Consideration, it was unanimously Agreed That, to prevent as much as possible their Attempting to return and molest the Settlers that may be set down on their Lands, it would be most proper to send them to be distributed amongst the several Colonies on the Continent…." Plans for rounding up the Acadians were made and officers of garrisons were sworn to secrecy to prevent forewarning and escape.

Colonel John Winslow, who was charged with the task of expelling the Acadians.

Exile

At Grand Pré, on Friday, September 5, Colonel John Winslow ordered his Massachusetts regiment to gather the Acadians together. Winslow ordered the Acadian men to assemble at the church to hear an important decree. The men came and were shocked when the decree to deport them was read. It bluntly stated "that your lands and tenements, cattle and live-

Reading the order of expulsion to the Acadians in the parish church at Grand Pré, in 1755, *by Charles William Jefferys. Like many modern portrayals, this is dramatic, if historically inaccurate.*

Above: The Embarkation of the Acadians, 1755, *another painting by Charles William Jefferys.*

Right: A modern illustraton of a Mi'kmaq warrior in clothing of European manufacture.

stock of all kinds are forfeited to the Crown, together with all your other effects, except money and household goods, and that you yourselves are to be removed from this His Province." The men were immediately surrounded by soldiers while other soldiers rounded up their families and torched their farms. For the next several weeks, the Acadians were kept under guard, awaiting deportation. Similar scenes unfolded at other Acadian villages. Squads of soldiers roamed the rural areas to bring all of the Acadians to ports where English ships would take them away. The removal of the Acadians began in October of 1755 and would continue over the next four years.

For 40 years the Acadians had been threatened with expulsion, but the English had never acted on their threats until now. At the eleventh hour, many Acadians appealed to the English. They would swear an unconditional oath if it would enable them to stay on their farms or in their fishing villages. But it was too late.

More than 2,000 Acadians were able to slip from the English grasp, but at least 7,000 were deported in the autumn of 1755 alone. Over 900 were shipped to Massachusetts, 955 to South Carolina, 860 to Maryland, 700 to Pennsylvania, 675 to Connecticut, 320 to Georgia, 290 to North Carolina and 200 to New York. Virginia refused to accept an allotment of 1,150 Acadians, for fear that they would somehow hinder the defence of that colony. These people were subsequently shipped to England. Many others were shipped back to France. The scheme was designed to transplant these French-speaking Catholics among large populations of English-speaking Protestants in the hopes that they would be assimilated into the larger populations. Acadia would be settled by English-speaking colonists to ensure its security in the war with France.

For the Acadians, this marked an extremely trying time in their history. Again, the experiences of the Daigle family mirrored the experience of thousands. They were rounded up in their various communities; Annapolis Royal, Grand Pré, Pisiquid, St. Charles de Mines and elsewhere and shipped to different locations. Those escaping the expulsion were helped by people of the Mi'kmaq Nation to avoid detection, but these refugees faced a harsh winter hiding out in the wilds of Nova Scotia or northern New Brunswick. Others escaped to Prince Edward Island or Louisbourg, only to be seized at these places later in the war and, like their former neighbours, forced into exile. By 1760, members of this close-knit family were in the interior of New Brunswick, in Quebec, England or France, or spread among several English colonies. Some of the young children died at sea on rough voyages into exile. Many of the older generation died within five years, perhaps from the rigours of the voyage or perhaps from the heartbreak of losing all that they had held dear. Those in the English colonies suffered greatly. English Protestant colonists showed their hatred for the Acadians as the war turned increasingly more vicious. Many Acadians eventually returned to their former home-

The Acadian deportation cross at Grand Pré, built in 1924 to commemorate the expulsion of the Acadians.

lands while others established a growing settlement in Louisiana. Hundreds more ended up in Quebec and stayed there while many families who had been shipped back to Europe never returned to the harsh realities of the New World. Typical of many Acadian families, there are thousands of Daigle descendents spread across the globe, with the largest numbers in New Brunswick and Louisiana but none on their original homesteads.

While the expulsion of the Acadians has given rise to many tales of suffering and the story is often looked at through modern eyes as a war atrocity, explusion was in fact standard procedure at the time when a conquered populace refused to swear fealty to the conqueror. It had been less than 10 years since English troops had slaughtered men, women and children in the Scottish highlands following the failed

1745–46 Jacobite war in a campaign of what would today be considered "ethnic cleansing." Although the expulsion was undoubtedly a tragedy, the Acadians were treated with remarkable leniency given the standards of the time.

By the end of the year, Braddock's grand scheme for 1755 was in tatters. Braddock himself had dismally failed to take Fort Duquesne and was killed in the effort; Shirley had not been able to launch his attack on Niagara; and Johnson, while gaining some success against the French in the Battle of Lake George, was not able to achieve the aim of that campaign, the capture of Fort Sainte-Frédéric. The Nova Scotia phase of the strategy was the only one that met with full success although the French remained firmly entrenched at the powerful Fortress of Louisbourg.

While many French, English and Native lives had been lost in the interior of the continent and great hardships were forced on the Acadians in the east, the war between England and France had still not been officially declared. That would come in the new year as the war in North America became more heated. Following Dieskau's defeat, the French quickly realized the importance of relying on tactics that had been the main characteristic of Native warfare for centuries, and which had been taught to the Canadiens by the Native war leaders. Henceforth, the regulars would use European-style tactics only when necessary and would increasingly heed the collective knowledge of the Canadiens and their Native allies. The English took a little longer to learn, and this would cost them dearly in the coming years.

3

THE FRONTIER WAR — 1756

"I must not lose sight of my design against Chouaguen (Oswego), since on the success of this depends the tranquility of the Colony."
— *Canadien Governor de Vaudreuil to the Minister of the Colonies, July 24, 1755*

Preparing for the 1756 Campaign

During the winter of 1755–56 France assembled reinforcements and supplies and appointed another experienced French general to replace Dieskau. In May the reinforcements and the new commander sailed from France in a flotilla of six ships. The 44-year-old Louis-Joseph, Marquis de Montcalm-Gozon de Sainte-Veran, veteran of many European campaigns, would make a lasting name for himself in the annals of Canada.

On May 18, 1756, war was finally officially declared between France and England, two years after hostilities began in North America. The Seven Years War, lasting until 1763, became a global conflict with

Louis-Joseph, Marquis de Montcalm sailed in 1756 to spearhead French North American operations.

battles fought in Europe, the West Indies and India, while the war continued to rage in the backwoods of North America. Through diplomatic manoeuvring which included heavy financial support for the Germans, the English were able to avoid sending English troops to Europe. They chose instead to fight their land wars in their far-flung empire and used the Royal Navy to battle the French in the Mediterranean, Atlantic and Indian oceans. This enabled them to concentrate more forces to fight the French in America and a new army was sent to the colonies under the Earl of Loudon.

Oswego — Montcalm's First Victory

The English planned a spring campaign that included an advance from Oswego on the southern shore of Lake Ontario to attack the French at Oswegatchie (Ogdensburg, New York) and Fort Frontenac (Kingston, Ontario). Montcalm would foil that effort.

At the English Fort Oswego, the garrison was suffering from scurvy, dysentery and starvation. The soldiers under Lieutenant-Colonel

A South View of Oswego on Lake Ontario in North America, published in London Magazine *in 1760.*

A View of Fort Oswego and Fort Ontario. *Many early illustrations were created from verbal reports, and tended to give American forts a very European, often medieval appearance.*

James Mercer were the victims of inefficient logistics and a precarious supply route up the Hudson River, over an isolated portage guarded by two small forts. On March 27, a French and Native raiding party overwhelmed Fort Bull at the west end of the Great Carrying Place portage, isolating Oswego and increasing the problems faced by its ailing garrison. Oswego would have to be relieved immediately to prevent its capture by the French. General Shirley ordered Lieutenant-Colonel John Bradstreet to raise a corps of boatbuilders and boatmen to secure the supply route to Oswego. Bradstreet was able to build boats in

The capitulation of Oswego in 1756. Montcalm's Native allies played a key role in capturing the garrison.

A Native headdress from the eastern Great Lakes region.

Guyenne and La Sarre, 1,500 experienced soldiers of the Compagnies franches de la Marine and Canadien militia, 80 pieces of artillery and 250 Native allies from several nations including Abenakis, Menomonees, Onondagas, Cayugas, Oneidas, Caughnawagas and Mississaugas.

Oswego was very poorly designed. The original stone blockhouse was built in 1727 where the Oswego River empties into Lake Ontario. It was now flanked by the new Fort Ontario, a small post 500 metres away on the far side of the river and a second redoubt perched on a small hill, a similar distance away on the other flank. The garrison of the three posts totalled 1,135 men, many of whom were still too ill to be effective.

After carefully scouting Oswego, Montcalm began formal siege operations on August 13, 1756, digging covered trenches in which to place artillery. Oswego's commander realized that the new Fort Ontario could not withstand a battering and abandoned that position prior to a French attack. On the following morning, Montcalm discovered that Fort Ontario was empty and moved his cannons into this fort, which overlooked Fort Oswego where the gun positions all pointed in the opposite direction. While the English were trying to heave their heavy guns around to face Fort Ontario, using pork barrels to build rudimentary covering defences, the French cannons opened fire. British Lieutenant-Colonel Mercer was beheaded by a French cannon ball early in the action and Lieutenant-Colonel John Littlehales assumed command of the beleaguered fort.

The French guns pounded the weakened British position, and soon Littlehales raised the white flag to surrender the garrison. While Montcalm tried to accept the surrender, many of his Native allies and Canadien militia swarmed into the post, quickly found the rum supply and just as quickly became senselessly drunk. During the chaos following the surrender, many of the sick and wounded in the hospital were murdered and

record time and successfully moved supplies to the grateful garrison. By June, the fort was strengthened, and two additional small forts were being worked on at the mouth of the river.

As the English were strengthening Oswego, Native scouts brought regular reports to Montcalm's headquarters. Montcalm was a man of action and after spending the early summer courting Native alliances, he left Montreal on July 25 at the head of a sizeable army bound for Oswego, more than 300 kilometres away. His army included 1,300 regulars of the Regiments Bearn,

A French medal struck to commemorate the capture of Oswego.

a number of soldiers and women and children at the fort were taken captive by Native warriors. Montcalm, unused to the violence of backwoods warfare and appalled at the capture of women and children, tried to restore order. He finally ended up buying captives back from some of the Native warriors and eventually put an end to the slaughter. In the end, as many as 100 English soldiers and civilians had been killed in both the artillery bombardment and the aftermath of the surrender and a number of women and children were taken away as captives to Native villages.

While Montcalm had been aware of tales of brutality in frontier warfare, he had not been prepared for the aftermath of the attack on Oswego. Many of the Native men with his force were from mission villages and were devout Roman Catholics. Montcalm assumed they would react to the surrender in the same manner as disciplined French regular soldiers. Ancient culture ran deeper than the imported religion, however, and the right of the warrior to take captives and belongings from a defeated enemy was foremost. In addition, Montcalm seemingly never understood that warriors were independent of the ideals of European military discipline. From highly individualistic societies, warriors could not be ordered to do anything. They chose to ally themselves with whom they wished when they

Etow Oh Koam, or Chief Nicholas. One of several paintings by John Verelst of one of the "Four American Kings," 1710.

wished but would never place themselves under the "command" of anyone. The capture of Oswego was a success. The French seized the supplies of the fort, burned the buildings and destroyed or seized the boats that had been assembled at Oswego. They took their booty and returned to Fort Frontenac. Montcalm's short campaign had ended any English threat to Fort Frontenac or Niagara for the foreseeable future.

When the Earl of Loudon received news of the fall of Oswego on August 20, he called off a planned campaign on Lake Champlain. At this point, relationships between the English and Native nations sank: the English just seemed to be too inept and the French appeared to be the dominant power on the continent. Native nations, very aware of the negative consequences of backing a loser, either joined the French cause outright or decided to remain neutral and keep an eye on the struggle until the probable outcome became clearer.

Native Warfare

While these military campaigns were occupying the main English and French forces in the Lake Champlain and Lake Ontario areas, the frontiers of Pennsylvania, Maryland and Virginia were sparsely defended. Following Braddock's defeat in the summer of 1755 and the seeming incompetence of the English during the summer of 1756, Native warriors felt secure in launching a bloody guerilla warfare campaign on the frontiers. War parties, often accompanied by French officers and Canadien militiamen, raided the isolated farms and settlements of the English colonies with increasing frequency and ferocity. Hundreds of settlers were killed or captured, hundreds of cabins and farms burned, and the frontiers of the colonies driven back to the Alleghenies.

By modern standards, Native warfare was vicious and brutal, a type of psychological warfare that filled the enemy with terror, rendering them panic-stricken and disorganized. The various Native nations of eastern North America had an extremely long history of war stretching back thousands of years. Hunting grounds and villages had to be continuously defended against encroachment by other nations. Men were raised as hunters and warriors and prestige went to the man who was successful in the hunt and victorious in war.

A number of concepts and practices that Europeans found "barbaric" or "savage" had developed within Native cultures. The need to avenge the dead to placate their souls was a powerful sentiment among them. War parties would try to capture enemy prisoners who could be brought back to the village and tortured or, increasingly more common, adopted into the families of those who had lost loved ones. The adoptee, then, would take the place of the dead loved one. By the time of the Seven Years War, adoption was far more common than torture. Many of the nations by that time, especially the people of the Six Nations and the men of the Seven Nations of Canada who lived closer to French settlements, had abandoned older violent practices and often acted as middle-men to prevent warriors from other nations from torturing their captives. This type of warfare was not usual among Europeans, who did not torture captives and usually did not kill prisoners, particularly women and children.

The terror instilled by the raids during the summer and autumn of 1756 caused many settlers to abandon their holdings and return to the towns of the eastern seaboard. It also made many men reluctant to join the army to fight against the French on extended campaigns for fear that their families would be left defenceless on the frontier. Thus, displaying the most effective principles of guerilla warfare, a relatively small number of Native warriors and French allies were able to keep the English colonies in a state of terror and confusion. The shock and brutality of this warfare, combined with the stealthy, lightning-quick raids, gave the Native warriors a fearful reputation. As the tales of these events unfolded, often exaggerated in the telling, English soldiers and provincials from the towns dreaded encounters with Native forces and were frightened and demoralized when marching through the forests of America. Braddock's defeat in 1755 and the "massacre" at Oswego in 1756, added to the reputation of the Native warriors and their French allies.

Reorganization in the English Colonies

As 1756 came to a close, Lord Loudon was proving his administrative skills. He had analysed the previous campaigns and realized that the whole system of mustering colonial soldiers, or "provincials" as they were known, and the system of organizing transportation and supplies for these armies was too cumbersome. Defensive measures were dependent on individual colonial legislatures voting money for paying for soldiers and supplies and for the transport of their own colonial armies.

Campaigns would be planned in the winter and spring but by the time the colonies had debated the issue, raised the money, mustered the troops, assembled the supplies and organized the transport, the campaign season would already be well advanced. Loudon set out to reorganize the system, initially to centralize the supply and transport function, and ultimately to centralize the raising and deployment of colonial troops.

Loudon was still busy reorganizing when he received new orders from William Pitt, whose recent appointment as secretary of state gave him the authority and responsibility of directing foreign affairs. Pitt took great interest in events in America and ordered a large military force and a large Royal Navy fleet to be sent to America. Loudon was ordered to seize the French fortress of Louisbourg and gain control over the mouth of the St. Lawrence River, thereby restricting supplies to New France. Loudon's plan, then, was set for 1757. He would hold the French on Lake George and capture the formidable fortress of Louisbourg. Or so he hoped.

4

MASSACRE AT FORT WILLIAM HENRY — 1757

"But spectacles still more frightening have befouled my eyes and left an ineffaceable bitterness in my soul."
— Montcalm's aide-de-camp, Louis-Antoine de Bougainville to his mother about the Fort William Henry Massacre, September 1, 1757.

The Richelieu River–Lake Champlain–Lake George corridor proved to be a convenient route between New England and New France. It was a vitally important strategic area for both belligerents from an offensive and defensive perspective. Following the Battle of Lake George in 1755, the French constructed a new fort on the river linking Lake George and Lake Champlain at a place known as the Ticonderoga Narrows or Crown Point. This fort, guarding the approaches to Fort Sainte-Frédéric, would be named Fort Carillon. The English similarly dug in and in the autumn of 1755, William Johnson ordered the construction of a small fort at his camp and named it Fort William Henry. During the ensuing winter, the French guarded the north end of Lake George while the English remained entrenched at the south end, each sending scouts out to reconnoiter the other's positions.

A 1776 painting of the old French fort of Carillon on Lake Champlain, which was taken by the English and renamed Fort Ticonderoga.

Marquis de Vaudreuil, the governor of New France, painted circa 1753–55.

Fort William Henry was an important staging post for any English advance against the French forts guarding the Lake Champlain–Richelieu River route. The French recognized the threat represented by this fort both as an English post from which an invasion could be launched and as a block to possible French attacks into New York.

When the Earl of Loudon arrived in America to take command, William Shirley had already laid plans for assembling an army at William Henry for an advance on the nearby French posts. Loudon's second-in-command, Major-General James Abercromby, was placed in command of this expedition but quickly ran into problems. His haughty bearing towards colonial soldiers demoralized the men already assembled at William Henry, and the cumbersome methods of gathering supplies by the fragmented colonies led to failure. By the time Abercromby had assembled enough men, munitions, supplies and transportation at William Henry, it was too late in the season to conduct the campaign. It would have to be postponed until the summer of 1757.

The First Siege of Fort William Henry

Shortly after arriving in New France, Montcalm had clashed with Governor Vaudreuil, who had been appointed to his position in 1755. Both men seemed jealous of each other's authority, and had

A modern illustration of a Compagnies franches de la Marine soldier in campaign dress, as he would have appeared at Fort William Henry.

differing views on how the defence of Canada should be conducted. During the winter, the conflict became critical and Vaudreuil

An 18th-century Native war club from the Great Lakes region.

took every opportunity to discredit Montcalm in dispatches to France. The bitterness that existed between the French regulars and the Canadiens mirrored the attitudes in the English colonies, where American provincials and legislators frequently had serious differences of opinion with English officers and generals.

In the late winter of 1757, Vaudreuil sought to win a victory for the Canadiens, developing a scheme to capture Fort William Henry. Vaudreuil's intention was to launch a surprise attack on the English fort, overwhelming it before the garrison became aware of the attack. It was correctly assumed that the garrison would be less vigilant during the winter months.

Vaudreuil's brother, Captain Rigaud de Vaudreuil, was chosen to lead a force of 1,600 Canadiens, Natives and Compagnies franches de la Marine soldiers to attempt to capture Fort William Henry. The Canadiens and their Native allies were used to winter travel, and by using ice skates, toboggans and snowshoes they were able to move quickly across the frozen Lakes Champlain and George towards the English fort. The French and Native force arrived near Fort William Henry on Friday, March 18, 1757, planning to attack the fort in the early hours of the following morning.

Things looked dim for Fort William Henry. The garrison of 400 regulars under Major William Eyre was poorly supplied and had neither fresh food nor warm clothing. Many of the men were suffering from dysentery, scurvy, smallpox and various winter ailments. The approaching force outnumbered them four to one. However, the fortifications were strong and the French, travelling light, had brought no heavy artillery with them. The French and Native force was discovered by the English, who quickly manned the ramparts. The French lost the advantage of a surprise attack. While the French and their Native allies burned a number of boats assembled by the English for the campaign planned for the following summer, they could not force a surrender of the garrison.

To the English, the defence of William Henry was regarded as a victory. In New France, Governor Vaudreuil also spoke of his brother's campaign as a success. In a way it was. With the English boats on Lake George destroyed, it would be difficult for them to launch an attack on Fort Carillon or Fort Sainte-Frédéric in the coming season.

The Fort William Henry Massacre

Where Captain Rigaud de Vaudreuil had failed by using typical frontier tactics against William Henry, Montcalm was determined to succeed using European ones. Montcalm began his preparations in May, ordering the Bearn and Royal Roussillon Regiments to Carillon. He also arranged to have food and supplies shipped there. Montcalm began a concerted effort to recruit as many Native allies as possible for the coming campaign, tirelessly visiting the villages and camps of numerous nations to explain his plans. More than 2,000 warriors from 41 nations soon bolstered his army. These men set up camps in the Lake Champlain area, where they joined six regular French regiments, the Compagnies franches de la Marine, Canadien militia and artillerymen with over 30 heavy cannons and 15 mortars. By the end of July, the French had also assembled a huge fleet of batteaux and canoes on Lake Champlain.

A fanciful representation of the Chevalier de Lévis.

On July 31, the Chevalier de Lévis was sent by land from Fort Carillon with 2,500 French soldiers and a few hundred Native allies towards Fort William Henry. Two days later, Montcalm's main force set out by water with 3,500 French and Canadien soldiers, 1,500 Native warriors and a formidable collection of artillery in a large fleet of canoes and batteaux, bound for William Henry. Montcalm's army rendezvoused with a force led by de Lévis near Fort William Henry on August 3, 1757, and prepared to capture the English post.

Fort William Henry was a relatively strong fort, flanked on one side by the lake and on another side by a swamp. Seventeen cannons bristled from its bastions while several mortars, which fired heavy exploding shells, were placed inside. An entrenched camp on a hillside east of the swamp covered the road to Fort Edward, only 20 kilometres away. The commander of the fort was a feisty Scot, Lieutenant-Colonel George Monro of the 35th Regiment of Foot, and the garrison consisted of 2,200 men, less than half of them English regulars. A number of the soldiers, regulars and provincials were married and many women and children were also inside the fort when the French began their attack.

Montcalm used classic siege warfare to attack the fort. His "sappers" began digging trenches through which his soldiers could safely approach and in which his artillery could be placed. As each protected gun battery position was prepared and heavy cannons moved within range of the fort,

An English trade gun.

the bombardment of William Henry gained in ferocity. Monro's cannons and mortars fired back but did little damage to the French positions as the siege lines slowly crept closer to the fort. Native allies, who because of their warfare methods would not participate in sieges, continually scouted the surrounding woods, prepared to ambush any English reinforcements.

Monro knew that it was only a matter of time until the French were able to capture the fort. He also knew that a large force of provincials was due to arrive at Fort Edward at any time and hoped to hold out until reinforcements arrived to break the French siege. He sent dispatches to General Daniel Webb, his commanding officer, who was entrenched at Fort Edward with 1,600 troops, begging the general to send a relief force immediately.

Webb was a cautious man, reluctant to help Fort William Henry until the expected provincials arrived to reinforce his own army. He did not wish to weaken Fort Edward and risk its garrison by hastily marching off to Monro's relief. The reports of the size of the French force were greatly exaggerated and Webb felt that attempting to advance towards the beleaguered fort would prove disastrous. His answer to Monro was a suggestion to capitulate and seek the best terms possible. The messenger carrying this response was ambushed on the road by Native warriors and the captured orders were eventually given to Montcalm. The French general sent his aide de camp, Louis-Antoine de Bougainville, under a flag of truce to speak with Monro. The French officer delivered the captured dispatch and again asked Monro to give up. Monro refused and the bombardment of Fort William Henry continued.

Things had become desperate inside the fort. Casualties had been heavy and, to make matters worse, an outbreak of smallpox was taking an increasing toll on the defenders. Monro finally decided to seek terms for surrender and sent an officer to Montcalm's camp to negotiate an end to the siege.

Montcalm was very generous, treating the surrender as one would in

A contemporary artist's impression of a Roger's Rangers officer.

Europe when an enemy has put up a gallant defence. The English were offered the "honours of war" and were to be permitted to march out of the fort beating their drums and carrying their regimental flags. They could take one field gun with them. They would be sent to Fort Edward if they agreed not to take up arms for the balance of the war or until "exchanged" with French soldiers similarly "paroled." Montcalm had also spoken with the Native leaders, getting their assurance that they would respect these terms. He did not want a repeat of the post-surrender chaos at Oswego, and was concerned that such atrocities would cloud his reputation.

However, as soon as the garrison of Fort William Henry marched out of the gates to join their comrades at a nearby fortified hillside camp, many Native warriors and Canadiens raced into the fort to grab what booty they could. Rum barrels were found and breached and the sick and wounded in hospital were killed and scalped. This mob then sped to the entrenched camp and began killing unarmed English soldiers and civilians. An outraged Montcalm rode to the scene, risking his life to stop the violence. Calm was eventually restored and Montcalm set a guard up in the camp while planning to send the English garrison to Fort Edward the following day with a protective escort.

On August 10, the refugees set out again, escorted by regulars and Canadien militia. Again Native warriors attacked the column, killing men, women and children and taking others captive for

A Six Nations sword belt. Swords were often given to Native war chiefs as gifts.

adoption. The Canadien escort did nothing to help, standing by to watch the slaughter. Again, Montcalm took action, riding to the scene to restore order. The column was finally reassembled and escorted to safety at Fort Edward by French regular soldiers. When the terrified garrison finally left the scene, as many as 100 scalped and mutilated bodies covered the ground. Another 200 people were missing, carried off into the forest by Native war parties.

The event represented a clash of cultures. To many Native nations, surrender was seen as a weakness and prisoners were killed outright, ritually tortured or adopted into the nation. The idea of allowing a defeated enemy to march away was not understood. It was the right of the warrior to gain the possessions of a vanquished foe and to take that enemy's life with no allowances for age or sex. Europeans followed the same convention in war when troops captured a town by force, and were just as guilty of such excesses, and worse, in Europe. However, because the English had surrendered and Montcalm had allowed them terms, the European mind was appalled by what happened on that August day in 1757 and Montcalm's reputation did indeed suffer as a result.

The event led Montcalm and his fellow European officers to mistrust their Native allies to some extent. They also looked at their Canadien comrades, who had participated in the looting, with different eyes, and some believed that the militia had actually incited the Natives to attack the surrendered garrison. Montcalm's aide-de-camp, Bougainville, wrote "that this abominable action of the Indians at Fort William Henry has accomplices among the people who call themselves Frenchmen; greed for gain, the certainty of getting very cheaply from the Indians all the goods they had pillaged, are the primary causes of a horror for which England will not fail

Montcalm at Fort William Henry, 1757. This late 19th-century impression dramatically illustrates Montcalm's efforts to save the English captives.

to reproach us for a long time to come."

Montcalm did not follow up his victory by continuing the campaign. He was aware that reinforcements had arrived at Fort Edward. Many of his Native allies had left the area, returning home with their prizes of war and captives or because they had felt insulted by Montcalm's behaviour towards them following the fort's capture. He decided to burn William Henry and return to Fort Carillon.

New York was shaken when news of the "massacre" spread. Initially, it was expected that a huge French army would advance down the Mohawk and Hudson rivers and that the entire colony would be in danger. Ranger patrols, however, were soon able to report that the French had retired to the other end of the lake. The story of the massacre continued to grow, enhanced with each telling, and with it the thirst for revenge grew as well. However, it was too late in the season to begin a campaign against the French and once again a stalemate set in for the fall and winter. In North America, English fortunes seemed to be at their lowest point. Things would change dramatically in the new year.

5

THE BEGINNING OF THE END FOR NEW FRANCE — 1758

"Canada has been saved by a miracle in these past three years; nothing but peace can save it now in spite of the efforts and talents of M. de Montcalm."
— *Montcalm's Commissariat Officer Doreil to the French Minister of War, October 1758*

A trade-silver brooch. This type of item was given by the French and English as a gift to Native leaders or used in trade by merchants.

While the French and their Native allies had inflicted severe defeats on the armies of England and the colonies for the past few years of the war, success came with a cost that proved crippling to the French war effort. While French regulars, Canadien militia and allied Native warriors pushed back the frontiers of the English colonies, France itself was fighting in Europe, India and the West and East Indies. English naval power was overwhelming the French around the globe. While France had few spare troops and little in the way of supplies to send to New France, the French government sent what it could to Montcalm. However, strong English fleets based at Halifax and in the West Indies made it difficult for the supply ships to reach New France, which had to rely primarily on its own resources.

For New France, the situation rapidly became desperate. Canadien militia had spent much of the growing season of 1757 on campaign. Their farms suffered and the harvests were greatly reduced as a result. On the Atlantic coasts, fishing boats had been captured or deterred from setting out from port by ships of the Royal Navy and consequently the supply of salted cod, a staple in New France, was depleted.

Similarly, with so many Native men, accompanied by their wives, on campaign with the French, food supplies from agriculture, hunting and fishing were dangerously low in Native villages. To make matters worse, booty and scalps taken from the smallpox hospital at William Henry had been carried back to numerous villages and the disease spread throughout the land, killing thousands and weakening the survivors. By the winter of 1757, food was so scarce in New France that troops were given horse meat. Bread rations were severely reduced. Food riots broke out in Montreal and Quebec, where the citizens petitioned government officials to supply food from government stores. Montcalm could barely keep his troops supplied, and large numbers of militiamen returned to their homes that winter and would not return to fight in the following year's campaign. They had to ensure that their families did not starve to death.

Sir Jeffery Amherst, painted in 1759. Amherst led the English forces in the assault on Louisbourg.

Not only food, but supplies of all sorts were short and the Native peoples were not given the customary gifts of gunpowder, weapons, tools, clothing and food. The English, on the other hand, had a much more stable supply system, and were able to offer all such gifts to any Native people who would come to their agents and declare their neutrality. New France's main strength, the alliance with numerous Native nations, was weakened by its inability to match the supplies of the English. It was a confusing time for the Native nations. The French were the better fighters but the English appeared to have more sustainable strength and better supply lines. It began to look as though the French might win the battles but that the English might win the war. Many Native people decided to remain neutral in the coming year to see which European nation might prevail.

During this period, the squabbles between Vaudreuil and Montcalm intensified. Montcalm accused Vaudreuil and Canadien authorities of corruption while the governor tried to discredit Montcalm. Letters were sent to the Minister of Marine slandering the general's reputation, claiming that Vaudreuil was responsible for the victories over the English during the previous campaign season. This mistrust was to have a very negative influence on the events of 1758.

In England, William Pitt, who was now the prime minister, recalled the Earl of Loudon, who had proven to be a good administrator but a poor general, and appointed Major-General James Abercromby to take charge of the war in America. The intention now was to totally defeat New France. Major-General Jeffery Amherst was ordered to attack Louisbourg while Abercromby was ordered to take Fort Carillon. At the same time, Brigadier-General John Forbes was directed to capture Fort Duquesne. This three-pronged

A 1759 sketch of James Wolfe by Brigadier-General George Townsend, who drew several unflattering caricatures of his commanding officer.

offensive, well equipped with arms, men and supplies, was meant to end the French menace in New York, end French influence among the Native nations of the Ohio Valley by capturing French bases there, and open up the mouth of the St. Lawrence River in preparation for a final attack on Quebec.

Louisbourg

For the campaign against Louisbourg, a large army was assembled in England. A colonial force of rangers and militia was mustered to join the assault. The Royal Navy had maintained a blockade of the fort during the winter of 1757, to attempt to seal the garrison in and prevent the French from resupplying or reinforcing it. It had been an effective blockade. During the winter it was said that "not a family had an ounce of flour in the house" and starvation had set in. In March, six French ships were able to run the blockade, enter Louisbourg harbour, and unload much-needed supplies of food and ammunition. Governor Chevalier Augustin de Drucour of Louisbourg had received reports of English forces gathering in the colonies for an attack on the fortress and received intelligence from Native allies of the coming campaign, so he prepared his defences as best he could with the resources available.

In early June, the people of Louisbourg saw a powerful English fleet of more than 140 vessels hove into view. General Jeffery Amherst had arrived to attack the fort. On June 8, English soldiers were loaded into boats and under the command of Brigadier-General James Wolfe began to row towards the French shore. French cannons thundered as they fired at the bobbing boats slowly approaching the shore. The fire proved too fierce and Wolfe ordered the boats to turn about. In doing so, they drifted east, where higher land protected

The barracks at Louisbourg, as they appear today.

cannons to return the English fire, but gradually the French gun positions were destroyed. Governor Drucour's strategy was to hold out until Louisbourg could be reinforced or the English fleet driven off. If they could hold out until winter, the English army would have to lift the siege.

The English had begun bombarding Louisbourg and the harbour's island cannon battery on June 20, and within a week the island battery was silenced, the French gun positions having been destroyed by accurate English cannon fire. This left the harbour vulnerable, although the six French warships anchored there provided some protection against the English fleet. To constrict access to the harbour, the French deliberately scuttled several civilian ships in its entrance.

The men of Louisbourg manned the cannons on the walls

them from the French bombardment. Turning his boats about again, Wolfe had his men rowed to shore. The French, loath to incur heavy casualties, conceded the English landing and retreated into the fortifications of Louisbourg. The English had been given a break. Wolfe was pleasantly surprised that they were able to land so easily in the end. He wrote, "in general, it may be said that we made a rash and ill-advised attempt to land, and by the greatest good fortune imaginable we succeeded." Wolfe would again make a "rash and ill-advised attempt to land" at Quebec a year later.

The English army now poured ashore, unloading heavy artillery. Cannons and mortars were dragged within range of the French fortress and the long siege of Louisbourg began. English "sappers and miners" dug trenches and artillery batteries to protect the gunners and infantrymen and as each cannon and mortar was sited, a tremendous bombardment was opened on the French positions.

Louisbourg's garrison of 3,000 regulars and 2,600 sailors and marines used the huge fortification's 250

A demonstration of French artillery at Louisbourg.

of the fort, formed fire brigades to snuff out fires in the city and formed repair parties to shore up the crumbling defences of the fort as the English bombardment increased. As the siege dragged on into July, the English trenches crept closer and the cannon fire became more accurate. Added to the pounding of the heavy English siege guns was the terror of exploding mortar shells. The heavy thirteen-inch mortars fired a 90-kilogram, hollow cast-iron shell, filled with an exploding charge. Lobbed into the town, the bombs went off with a terrific explosion, scattering large chunks of iron fragments and levelling any wooden building that they chanced to hit. On July 6, one of the bombs, fired in a high trajectory from the English lines, crashed through the roof of the hospital and exploded, killing several men, including a surgeon, and wound-

A modern illustration of French regular soldiers pausing as a civilian woman gives them a drink. Louisbourg's citizens suffered terribly under the massive English bombardment.

ing many of the patients.

For the civilians of Louisbourg, this was a terrifying experience. No place inside the fortification was safe and the English shelling continued without pause, night and day. As the defences on the west wall crumbled under fire, work gangs laboured to fill the gaps and conduct hasty repairs. One of the French officers reported that "houses had to be torn down for wood to repair fortifications and such work had to be carried out under a fire which swept not only the defences but the streets of the town." Each morning, the sleepless people of Louisbourg emerged from

their crude shelters, looked out to sea and noted the huge English fleet. Towards the land, they could see the English trenches zig-zagging closer to the wall of the fort as the English laboured to extend the approaches.

On July 15, the people were somewhat cheered to note that one of the French warships in the harbour was able to escape, miraculously running the English blockade and making a run for the open sea. The beleaguered people of Louisbourg hoped that the ship could deliver word of their plight and perhaps a French force would be sent to their relief. The fortress was doomed, however, and would soon be forced to surrender. By this time, many of the French cannons had been silenced. Ammunition for the undamaged guns was getting dangerously low and the civilians were

The burning of French ships in Louisbourg harbour during the siege, painted circa 1770.

now gathering English cannon balls from inside the town to bring to the French gunners, who could fire at least some of the projectiles back at their enemies.

On July 21, disaster struck. A cannon shot struck one of the French ships in the harbour, igniting cannon cartridges on its deck. The resulting fire crossed to another of the French ships, which began to burn fiercely. Then, a third ship started to burn. As the fire became fiercer, heavy billows of foul smoke blew inland, smothering the town. Governor Drucour later wrote of the effect on the people of Louisbourg:

"The few casemates [subterranean, bomb-proof structures] are placed in the inner part of the citadel, in them were shut in the ladies and some of the women of the town, and one was kept for wounded officers. There was every reason to fear that the fire would reach the protection which had to be placed in front of the casemates, and by the direction of the wind the smoke might stifle the women shut up in them, so that all the women and a great number of little children came out, running to and fro, not knowing where to go in the midst of bombs and balls falling on every side."

The timing could not have been worse for the people thus forced from shelter. In the harbour, the cannons aboard one of the fiercely burning vessels fired off in the heat, sending a number of cannon balls crashing into the crowd of civilians. Another of the ships blew up in a terrific explosion as the flames reached its powder magazine.

By July 22, the English were firing more than 300 mortar shells daily into the disintegrating fort. They were now close enough to fire incendiary devices into the town, setting fire to the blasted buildings and trying the limits of those who tried to douse the flames. Every building in Louisbourg had been badly damaged or completely destroyed by this stage but still the French held on.

On the morning of July 25, under the distraction of an incredible bombardment of the town, English sailors rowed into the harbour and captured the last two French warships. They sailed one out of the harbour and then set the other on fire. This was the last straw. The French were exhausted and totally demoralized by this final defeat. They now knew that nothing could prevent the English fleet from entering the harbour, where their hundreds of heavy cannons could level the fort.

On the following day, Drucour surrendered the fort unconditionally. The civilians and some of the soldiers dreaded what would happen next. Many of the people were badly wounded, food was in extremely short supply, and disease was taking its toll on the survivors. Hanging over everyone's head was the knowledge of the excesses of the French troops and their allies following the surrender of Oswego in 1756 and Fort William Henry in 1757. Among the French troops were men of the "Wild Geese," Irishmen who had taken service in the army of France, who feared that the English would hang them as traitors. When the smoke cleared, the defending troops and the terrified inhabitants were greatly relieved to discover that the English had no intention of taking revenge. The garrison was paroled and shipped back to France while many of the civilians suffered the same fate as the earlier Acadian populations. Others were able to escape and found refuge in the interior of the colony. Some made it to Quebec, where they were able to spread the word of the horror of living under siege but also of the generous terms offered by the English on the surrender of the fortress. This may have had an impact on the population of Quebec the following year, when they endured a similar lengthy siege.

Following the consolidation of their prize, the English sent a force to capture St. Anne and Spanish Bay (Sydney) and to confront the French at Prince Edward Island. The island quickly surrendered and its population of more than 3,000 people were expelled. From the end of August to the end of September, English soldiers landed from ships at French outposts and villages in New Brunswick. Fishing boats, farms, villages and forts were burned by the English under the command of James Wolfe. The people who could be rounded up were exiled.

Many, however, were able to escape into the woods to take refuge in Mi'kmaq settlements, where they would wait to return to their land. Wolfe wrote of the bitter experience of this devastation of the Atlantic coast, an act that was considered important for the following year's campaign against Quebec. "We have done a great deal of mischief; spread the terror of His Majesty's arms through the whole gulf, but added nothing to the reputation of them."

The route to Quebec now lay open.

The embarkation of Abercromby's expedition against Fort Carillon, July, 1758. Another dramatic, but not totally historically accurate, early 20th-century portrayal.

Fort Carillon

While Amherst was slowly destroying Louisbourg through the use of classical siege warfare, General Abercromby was preparing a poorly conceived frontal assault against Fort Carillon to clear the French from the Lake Champlain area. Abercromby assembled his regulars and provincials and marched to the camping ground on Lake George near the ruins of Fort William Henry. Sir William Johnson, who had been performing incredible feats of diplomacy to convince the Six Nations to support this campaign on the Lake George–Lake Champlain front, joined him here. With Johnson were about

400 Six Nations warriors who were still willing to assist the English against the French. A base camp was set up and supplies stockpiled. Like Lord Loudon before him, Abercromby was a brilliant quartermaster and administrator but a poor tactician with little appreciation for frontier tactics or for assaults on fortified positions. For this role, he was blessed by the presence of his subordinate, Brigadier-General Lord George Howe.

General Howe took what little time was available to train English regulars to fight like the provincials, using tactics which had proven essential in wilderness warfare. Methods perfected by Roger's Rangers and other effective backwoods

A view of Fort Ticonderoga, painted in 1759 by Thomas Davies, an English officer who participated in the fort's capture from the French.

rangers, moved in advance of the main force to scout ahead and prevent any ambushes. Howe proved very popular among the soldiers and his presence in the army raised morale and confidence considerably. However, on July 8, Lord Howe was killed in a brief skirmish with a French advance guard which then quickly vacated an outpost near the site of the English landing to retreat to the safety of Carillon. Robert Rogers, writing of Howe's death, said that "the fall of this noble and brave officer seemed to produce an almost general languor and consternation through the whole army." Without Howe's superior tactical skills, Abercromby's campaign was doomed to failure, in spite of his overwhelming advantage in troop numbers.

warriors were taught to the redcoats, whose training until that time had been in the strict, well-drilled linear tactics common on open European battlefields but ineffective in dense woods. The superb fighting men of the Six Nations contingent served as excellent role models during this training. The soldiers were also ordered to travel light, cutting their voluminous coats and hats into trim garments that would be less likely to snag in the thick woods and trading their largely decorative short "hangers" or swords for the more practical belt axe or tomahawk.

Abercromby had ordered boat builders to the site of Fort William Henry in the spring to build a flotilla that would replace those vessels destroyed by the French in the capture of the fort the previous year. By early July, Abercromby had assembled an army of 6,000 regulars and 9,000 provincials on the shores of Lake George. On July 6, the army was embarked on batteaux, barges and small sailing vessels and began to sail up Lake George towards the French position. On landing on the far side of the lake, only six kilometres from the French Fort Carillon, Brigadier-General Howe, with his trained light infantry soldiers and various companies of

An 18th-century Six Nations shot pouch.

In Quebec, the French had learned of Abercromby's intentions by late spring. French and Native patrols kept an eye on the English settlements and forts and Montcalm received accurate reports of Abercromby's moves. In response, Montcalm ordered his French regulars to Lake Champlain to bolster the defences of Forts Sainte-Frédéric and Carillon and begged Vaudreuil to call out the militia and order them to the Lake Champlain area. Vaudreuil complied, although with no great

Six Nations re-enactors pictured at Fort Niagara in 2001. Abercromby's Native allies were appalled by his careless tactics at Fort Carillon.

haste. Montcalm then travelled to Fort Carillon to take personal command of the troops. Even when Montcalm had all of these men gathered by July 8, he still had only slightly more than 3,500 men, most of them regulars, to oppose Abercromby's army of 15,000. Montcalm planned to put up a spirited defence of Carillon, delaying the English long enough to allow the bulk of the militia and Native allies to join him there. He hoped that a protracted action would last long enough so that the season would be too far advanced for an English attack on Quebec, presuming that they were eventually able to capture the French positions on Lake Champlain. He put his men to work digging trenches on the land side of Fort Carillon, which was protected on three sides by the waters of the Ticonderoga Narrows. His men cut down trees and sharpened their branches and limbs, entangling the branches together facing the direction from which the English would have to attack. This defensive work, or "abatis," like barbed wire in later wars, was simple but effective against infantry, although any force using siege artillery could quickly destroy it.

Abercromby's army arrived before Carillon on August 9 and the general immediately ordered an assault. He would not wait to bring up his cannons, still back at the landing place. English and Native scouts scanned the French defences and reported the difficult tangle of abatis to Abercromby, but also noted the small size of the French garrison defending the fort. Abercromby's force outnumbered Montcalm's by four to one, so he ordered his regulars forward. English skirmishers drove the French piquets, or sentries, back behind the defences and then the English infantry attacked. Eight thousand redcoats, bayonets fixed, charged the French position but they could not penetrate the abatis. French soldiers fired volley after volley into the stalled attackers, causing heavy casualties.

For the English soldiers, Carillon was a place of horror. Time after time, Abercromby ordered the soldiers to attack with the same results. In frustration, the fierce highlanders of the Black Watch attacked in a "highland charge," swinging their sharp claymore swords as they tried to scramble over the abatis. Caught in the tangle of trees, vainly hacking at the branches with their claymores, the men were cut down before they could reach the French soldiers on the other side.

By nightfall, more than 1,000 English had been killed or wounded. Abercromby ordered his men back to Lake George, where his defeated army was re-embarked to return to the staging area at Fort William Henry. Montcalm's stalwart little army and the incredibly effective abatis, as well as Abercromby's haste to launch a frontal attack without artillery support, had assured that Quebec would be safe for another year.

The effect on the precarious Native alliance was severe. The Six Nations people who had witnessed Abercromby's blundering attack were disgusted with the waste of human lives and returned to their villages to reassess their alliance with the English. Much of Sir William Johnson's tireless diplomatic work among the Six Nations had been destroyed in a few hours at Carillon.

Fort Frontenac

Montcalm's defence of Carillon had left Fort Frontenac (Kingston, Ontario) lightly guarded. The cannons at this post were old and many had been condemned as worthless. While

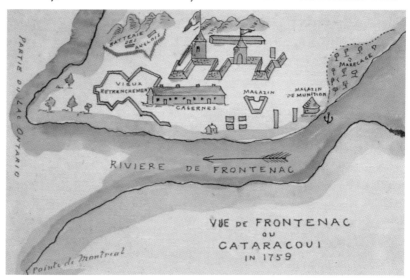

A 1759 plan of Fort Frontenac. The French surrendered the fort without a shot being fired.

A 19th-century impression of the evacuation of Fort Duquesne. After his Native allies left for home, French commander de Lignery had no choice but to burn the fort and retreat.

Montcalm was keeping a wary eye on the Lake Champlain front, another English force was moving to take advantage of the French weakness at Frontenac. Lieutenant-Colonel Bradstreet, a man who had learned the value of provincial soldiers and of the methods of frontier warfare, assembled an army that moved up the Hudson and Mohawk rivers and across the Great Carrying Place and eventually to the site of Oswego. He then sailed and rowed across Lake Ontario in late August and landed near Fort Frontenac on August 26. The English and Native force quietly deployed during the morning of August 27 until they had the fort surrounded, apparently undetected by the small French garrison of about 100 men under Captain de Noyen. When his men were in place, Bradstreet demanded the surrender of the fort and de Noyen had no choice but to comply. Bradstreet's men burned the fort, destroyed whatever stores they could not carry off and broke the "trunnions" off of the heavy cannon barrels, thus making them unserviceable. They carried off their booty in

two captured French schooners to return to Oswego, burning the remaining French vessels at Frontenac.

The destruction of Fort Frontenac and the loss of their schooners threatened the French supply route to Niagara, Detroit and, ultimately, to Fort Duquesne. It also created the possibility of an English thrust down the St. Lawrence River to threaten Montreal. Abercromby would not exploit this victory, however, making no commitment to attack Montreal or Niagara so late in the campaign season.

The Fall of Fort Duquesne

While Abercromby was wasting his army at Carillon, another English officer, Brigadier-General John Forbes, was slowly advancing to put the third prong of Pitt's strategy into effect, the capture of Fort Duquesne. Forbes assembled an army of some 6,000 men including 1,200 regulars, more than 4,600 provincials and several dozen allies from the Cherokee nation.

A General View of Quebec, from Point Levy, by Richard Short, 1761. Short was an English officer who was with Wolfe's army at the Plains of Abraham.

French Fort Le Boeuf, closer to Lake Erie and Fort Detroit.

On November 25, Forbes finally arrived at the destroyed fort. He set his men to work to re-fortify the spot, naming the new post Fort Pitt, after the English prime minister. It would later become Pittsburgh.

Montcalm's Dilemma

At the close of 1758, the writing was on the wall for New France. Louisbourg was captured, Fort Duquesne had been taken and was now an English fort, Fort Frontenac had been put out of action, an English presence was re-established at Oswego, and the Native alliances which had been their main strength in the first years of the war were now weakened to the breaking point.

Throughout the summer and into the autumn, his army had slowly advanced through the wilderness, setting out from Philadelphia in June, cutting a wide road through the forests and stopping at intervals to build strong supply bases.

The French commander, Captain François-Marie Le Marchand de Lignery of the Compagnies franches, received frequent reports of the English advance. His garrison was small and his supplies were low. As the autumn approached, many of his Native allies drifted away from the area to return home to hunt and to see their families.

In mid-September, Major James Grant took an advance reconnaissance force to Fort Duquesne and attempted to capture the fort in a daring frontal assault. Grant's force was beaten back, suffering heavy casualties. This successful action against Grant gave the French only a short reprieve, however. Even more of their Native allies, feeling that they had now helped the French as much as possible with the campaign, left for home following the defeat of Grant's force, leaving the garrison of Duquesne very weak. The English army continued to slowly advance in spite of the lateness of the season. In late November, Lignery had the fort blown up to prevent its use by the English and retreated with his garrison to the smaller

Montcalm had a serious problem on his hands. Quebec had been isolated and was now threatened from three directions; down the St. Lawrence from Oswego, up the river from Louisbourg and the along the vulnerable Lake Champlain route. The troops defending New France had fought well but casualties had mounted and few replacements were available. The Native alliance was shaky and poor harvests tied the militia to their farms. Food, weapons and munitions were in short supply. Montcalm, victorious against the English in each of his campaigns, now spoke only of delaying the inevitable defeat of New France, hopefully long enough for peace to be negotiated in Europe before the English were finally able to overwhelm the French in North America. He knew that France would never be able to send sufficient reinforcements and supplies to prevent the eventual defeat of the colony. He wrote: "I am resolved to stand by it [New France] to the last and will bury myself under its ruins if need be…. I must do what I can to help it and retard its fall."

6

THE CONQUEST — 1759

"Come each death-doing dog who dares venture his neck,
Come, follow the hero that goes to Quebec.
Jump aboard of the transports and loose every sail,
Pay your debts at the tavern by giving leg-bail.
And ye that love fighting shall soon have enough,
Wolfe commands us, my boys, we shall give them
Hot Stuff."
— *Song written by Ned Botwood, killed at Quebec*
on July 31, 1759.

The winter of 1758–59 was dismal for the prospects of New France. Louisbourg, Fort Duquesne and Fort Frontenac had fallen to the English. The distant French forts of Niagara, Detroit, Michilimackinac and smaller posts were isolated with few supplies getting through to sustain the garrisons. Further, the storehouses of gifts for Native allies were practically empty. In the late autumn of 1758, the English had held successful treaty talks with the Delaware, Shawnee, Mingo, Wyandot and other nations, finally convincing most of their warriors to remain neutral as the war continued. Throughout French Canada, supplies of food were exhausted and many inhabitants were starving. Political dissension, dividing the leadership into two camps, one supporting Montcalm and the other supporting the governor, acted to further demoralize the Canadiens. Montcalm and Vaudreuil continued to send letters to their respective ministers, each accusing the other

A contemporary illustration of a Compagnies franches de la Marine soldier.

of incompetence or corruption. Knowledge of this conflict lowered morale among the officers of the regular forces and the militia of New France.

It was clear that more troops and more supplies were urgently required if New France was to stave off conquest in the coming year. Montcalm's aide-de-camp, Louis-Antoine de Bougainville, was sent to France in the early winter to beg the French government to forward the needed supplies.

Unfortunately, the war was going poorly for the French in Europe, India and elsewhere in their far-flung empire and little could be spared for the wilderness war in North America. Bougainville returned to Quebec in the spring with a scant reinforcement of a few hundred troops and three transport ships of supplies. The Canadiens and the regular French soldiers felt as though they were being abandoned by their mother country and this caused a further decrease in morale.

The Siege of Quebec

Bougainville also brought the unwelcome news that the English were arming a fleet for an assault on Quebec. It was rumoured that an army of 50,000 was on its way to finally take Canada. Montcalm had command of only 3,500 regular troupes de terre and 1,500 Compagnies franches de la Marine soldiers. While he could call on the support of about 13,000 Canadien militia, including very

A 1765 portrait of Admiral Charles Saunders, commander of the English fleet that laid siege to Quebec. The fleet was the largest assembled in North America prior to the 20th century.

young and very old men, few of them were trained in the type of European tactics that would surely be required to defend Quebec. Montcalm left small garrisons at Niagara, Carillon, Sainte-Frédéric and other posts, concentrating most of his men around Quebec. By the late summer of 1759, he had 3,000 regulars and 10,000 militia at the capital and posted at various points along the St. Lawrence River within a couple of days march.

In June, a huge English fleet under the command of Admiral Charles Saunders entered the St. Lawrence River. It was guided by navigator Captain James Cook, who would later make his name as an explorer, and piloted by Canadien river men hired, or forced, to find safe passages up the river for the fleet. This naval force was massive, including 50 warships bristling with cannons and more than 150 transport and troopships. On board were 8,500 regular army soldiers and tough American rangers under the command of Major-General James Wolfe, who had distinguished himself the previous year at the capture of Louisbourg. There were 13,000 sailors manning the ships and more than 600 marines, skilled in amphibious operations. Any Canadiens watching Saunders' fleet pass by must have been filled with terror. The huge fleet, the largest ever assembled in North America, stretched 80 kilometres as it ascended the St. Lawrence River. It would have taken at least 12 hours to pass any given point.

Wolfe's army disembarked at Île d'Orléans on June 26 and began reconnoitering the enemy position. They captured

Point Lévi, directly across the St. Lawrence from Quebec and began constructing gun batteries and fortified camps. Supply ships were unloaded and soon orderly tent cities sprang up with more than 3,000 white canvas tents pitched, latrines dug, and artillery parks laid out. The English had strict regulations regarding the layout of encampments, and the men were very efficient at setting out these very formal fortified camps. Soon, they established a third camp on the east side of the Montmorenci River, which separated the English position from the main French entrenchments. All of this activity — English ships filling the river, boats rowing to shore, tents springing up like mushrooms and the vast number of soldiers landing on the islands — would have been very visible from the ramparts of Quebec and undoubtedly caused many of the defenders to lose heart. Large siege guns and heavy bomb-firing mortars were quickly emplaced, and a bombardment of Quebec that would last for 10 weeks quickly commenced. Wolfe's plan was to try to destroy the city's defences and demoralize its defenders while awaiting reinforcements who would advance up the Richelieu River after capturing Carillon and Fort Sainte-Frédéric.

An English encampment, similar to the one that would have been pitched at Quebec, created by a re-enactment group at Fort Niagara.

The Capture of Lake Champlain

While Wolfe's army was preparing to bombard Quebec, a second English army was being led from Albany by the commander-in-chief of the English in North America, General Jeffery Amherst, the victor of Louisbourg. His army of 11,000 regulars and provincials travelled across Lake George, arriving near Fort Carillon in late July. Fort Carillon's garrison was only 2,000 men under the command of Brigadier-General François-Charles de Bourlamaque, who had remained there since the defeat of Abercromby the previous year.

With few Native allies accompanying his force, Bourlamaque knew that he could not stop the careful Amherst with the type of tactic used against the bungling Braddock or Abercromby. He destroyed the defences of Carillon and retreated to Fort Sainte-Frédéric, which he also destroyed, then finally fell back to Île-aux-Noix in the Richelieu River. His troops strengthened that fort's defences, moving cannons to face the line of the expected English advance. The French also slung heavy chains across the river to prevent English vessels from advancing past Île-aux-Noix to outflank their artillery batteries.

Amherst reached the site of Fort Carillon on July 23 and ordered some of his men to begin repairing the defences. This strategic stronghold was renamed Fort Ticonderoga. The English continued to advance, arriving at the site of Fort Saint-Frédéric on August 4. This site was also made into an English fort and would henceforth be known as Crown Point.

Amherst then sent a small force to scout the next leg of the route. They found that Île-aux-Noix had been well fortified. They also noted the presence of four small, armed French schooners, which would make the assault on the island by boat impossible. Amherst would need to set up shore batteries to bombard the fort and destroy these schooners before he could contemplate an amphibious assault on Île-aux-Noix. His provincial forces were getting anxious to return home with the approach of the harvest season, and Amherst realized that he would need another month or two to capture the island. He decided to cut his campaign short, leaving strong garrisons at Crown Point and Ticonderoga.

The Fall of Niagara

The third English army on the move in the summer of 1759 was led by Brigadier-General John Prideaux who mustered 5,500 regulars and provincials at Albany in June and set out to capture Fort Niagara. As they moved up the Mohawk River, Sir William Johnson and more than 600 Six Nations allies joined them. Together they slowly travelled by foot and by boat down the Oswego River, arriving at Oswego on June 27. Prideaux ordered 1,300 men to remain here, under the command of Frederick Haldimand, to improve the defences and to guard the lake to ensure that the French could not reinforce Niagara from Quebec.

The main force then boarded batteaux and set off along the south shore of Lake Ontario, landing at the Four Mile Creek near Fort Niagara on July 6. Prideaux's men immediately began to build a fortified camp at the landing place while scouts led engineers within site of the French fort to start a formal siege. On July 9 the English began digging "approaches, saps and parallels," the zigzag trenches that were the hallmark of European-style siege opera-

The "maison a machicoulis," or defensible house, built by the French at Fort Niagara in 1726. The building withstood battles in 1759 and 1813, though in both cases it was captured by English forces.

tions, to enable the army to slowly approach under cover. At the same time, batteaux were carried through the forest and launched on the Niagara River, upstream and out of sight of Fort Niagara. The boats carried heavy cannons and gunners to the west side of the river, and the guns were hauled a few kilometres to Montreal Point (now Mississauga Point in Niagara-on-the-Lake) directly opposite Fort Niagara. Soldiers began digging gun emplacements and felling trees for cannon platforms.

By July 17, all was ready. The trenches had been advanced and guns and mortars were placed in them and in batteries built at Montreal Point. Prideaux's force of more than 4,000 provincials and regulars was ready for the attack as soon as the cannons and mortar fire could breach the French defences. Sir William Johnson's army of Native

Sir William Johnson saving a French officer at Fort Niagara in 1759. This was painted to show that Johnson had more influence over his allies than did Montcalm at the surrender of Oswego and William Henry.

warriors had grown to almost a thousand men. The French commander of Fort Niagara, Captain Pierre Pouchot, was hopelessly outnumbered. Defending Fort Niagara were 149 regulars of the troupes de terre, 183 men of the Compagnies franches de la Marine, 133 militiamen and 21 artillerymen. There were also a number of civilians in the fort: 34 men, 5 women and 23 children.

On July 17, Prideaux's cannons and mortars began a devastating bombardment while his sappers continued to dig approach trenches. The French cannons fired back, but were gradually being put out of action by the English fire as casualties mounted inside the fort. There were losses on the English side as well. On the night of July 20, Prideaux was in one of the forward trenches observing the effect of the gunfire. A small coehorn mortar was fired from the English trench as Prideaux strolled in front of an artillery piece, killing the commanding general instantly. The leadership of the siege of

Fort Niagara now fell to Sir William Johnson.

Early in this campaign, when Pouchot's Native allies had given him intelligence of the English approach to Niagara, Pouchot had sent messages to the French western posts of Detroit, Venango and Le Boeuf in the Lake Erie area, asking for reinforcements. He also had sent agents to the western side of the Niagara River to seek help from the Mississauga Nation, but this proved unsuccessful. While the lack of response by the Mississaugas was disappointing, the Native warriors of the Detroit and Ohio areas continued to stand by their old alliances. A relief force from the western posts — 800 soldiers and 600 Native allies under the command of Captains Lignery and Aubry — was rapidly approaching Niagara.

Sir William Johnson learned of the approach of the French relief force and, while maintaining the siege, set up a strong defensive position close to Fort Niagara at a place called La Belle Famille, blocking the approach to the fort. Pouchot got word through to Lignery, suggesting that the relief force cross the Niagara to attack Montreal Point, but Lignery either did not receive the dispatch or ignored it. Instead, the relief force directly attacked the English and Native position at La Belle Famille on August 24. Lignery's force was defeated with very heavy casualties.

On learning of the English victory at La Belle Famille, Pouchot realized that all was hopeless. He sent a flag of truce to Johnson and negotiated terms that would allow the French to surrender with the "honours of war." Johnson accepted and, on August 25, Niagara surrendered. The French marched out in parade-like order carrying their muskets and dragging one cannon with their regimental colours flying and their drummers beating. As they boarded the English boats that would carry them into captivity, they piled their muskets on the shore. During the Seven Years War, captured officers could give their word not to fight rather than being imprisoned by their captors. When a number of officers of the opposing army had similarly been captured and given their promise, or "parole," they could be "exchanged," permitting them to return to active duty. The officers of Niagara gave their parole and were later exchanged, eventually returning to their army to fight again in the following year.

Desperate to break the English siege of Quebec, the French lit ships on fire and floated them toward the massive English fleet. This painting is a 20th-century rendition.

Bombardment of Quebec

At Quebec, Wolfe's army laboured to build well-protected gun batteries at Point Lévi and Île d'Orléans. While they were being built, the guns of Quebec continued to fire at the English positions and on the English fleet anchored just out of range in the St. Lawrence River. At the same time, bands of Canadien militia and Native warriors harassed the English army, ambushing any soldiers who

A 1797 impression of the English taking Quebec. Wolfe's men can be seen climbing the steep embankment toward the Plains of Abraham.

The walls of Quebec, 2001.

watch the opening shots. When large splashes in the river showed that the guns were firing short, the crowd cheered, thinking the English had built their batteries out of range, almost two kilometres from the city. They were soon disabused, however, as a mortar bomb arched through the air, exploding on the Jesuit Church. The people quickly fled, but there was no place to hide as solid shot ricocheted off of stone buildings and bombs detonated with loud concussions and flying iron shards. As the bombardment continued during the weeks following, most of the populace took refuge in the upper town. This did not provide much protection. One of the English eyewitnesses wrote in his journal on July 16 that "at eleven o'clock a fire broke out in a large building in the upper town, and burned with great fury, by the winds blowing fresh at north-west; the great cathedral church of Quebec with all its paintings, images and ornaments, were utterly destroyed." In the lower town, many of the buildings were made of wood. On August 10, a mortar bomb started a fire in the lower town that spread quickly and by the end of the day, half of the buildings there had been destroyed.

The destruction to Quebec was as great as that of any

strayed from the main camps. The French also tried to drive off the fleet by towing fire ships and rafts into the river with the intention of setting fire to the English ships. These ships and rafts, stocked with loaded cannons, barrels of pitch and tar, and boxes of hand grenades on their decks, were set on fire and cut adrift. They were a fearsome sight, with flames shooting up the masts, guns firing and grenades exploding, but the threat came to naught as some ran aground before reaching the English fleet, while others were towed out of harm's way by sailors in boats.

None of these actions stopped the completion of the batteries that opened fire on July 12 with a terrific bombardment of the defences and town of Quebec. On the first day of the bombardment, hundreds of solid cast-iron cannon balls, 96 large exploding mortar bombs and seven "carcasses" (incendiary devices) were fired at the town. During the next two months, the English would use 20 tons of gunpowder to fire more than 36,000 heavy cannon balls and 6,000 bombs into the beleaguered city with devastating effect.

When the bombardment began, a number of the townsfolk rushed to the ramparts to

Another painting by English officer Richard Short in 1761. The bombardment of Quebec was as devastating as any modern aerial attack would be.

Montmorenci Falls. The French drove an English invasion force back from here in July, 1759.

modern aerial bombardment. John Knox, an English soldier, visited Quebec after its capture. He wrote: "I had the opportunity of viewing more distinctly the great effect our artillery had upon it … and indeed the havoc is not to be conceived. Such houses as are standing are perforated by our shot, more or less; and the low town is so great a ruin that its streets are almost impassable." In the upper town, he noted: "their principal public buildings were the cathedral, of which only the walls remain; the bishop's palace, the colleges of the Jesuits and Récollets, the convents of the Ursulines and Hôtel-Dieu, with their churches, a seminary for the education of youth, almost beat to pieces, with a neat chapel adjoining; a stately but unfinished house for the Knights-Hospitallers, the intendant's magnificent palace in the suburb of St. Rocque and the church of Madame la Victoire [Notre-Dame des victoires] in the low town, of which the walls only are standing."

The bombardment destroyed the city and caused incredible hardship but did not force a surrender, and after the first two weeks of shelling, Wolfe realized that he would have to assault the fortress. On July 31, Wolfe launched an attack on the main French camp near the Montmorenci Falls. It went well for the English at first, with the army disembarking on the mud flats in front of the French fortifications and advancing in an orderly fashion. When the French skirmishers in front of the fortifications hastily withdrew under heavy gunfire, the headstrong English grenadiers, the tallest and toughest men of each regiment, previously grouped together by Wolfe into a body known as the "Louisbourg Grenadiers," mistook the quick withdrawal as a general retreat and raced after the French, losing all cohesiveness and preventing the guns of the English fleet from targeting the French. As the English grenadiers floundered in the mud, the French fired heavy musket volleys from behind their fortifications, causing severe casualties among the grenadiers. Finally, the English retreated back to their boats and rowed away. The bombardment of Quebec continued as Wolfe looked for other avenues of attack.

Collateral Damage

The campaign for Quebec was total war, with civilians suffering as much as the soldiers guarding the city. The scene seemed idyllic before the assault began. One of Wolfe's officers described the scene as the fleet approached Quebec in June: "Here we are entertained with a most agreeable prospect of a delightful country on every side; windmills, water-mills, churches, chapels and compact farm-houses, all built with stone and covered, some with wood and others with straw. The lands appear to be every-where well cultivated…." For the Canadiens living on these farms and in these villages, the next three months would be a time of terror.

It was standard practice in war at the time for an occupying army to make free use of any civilian structures for shelter. With each soldier consuming 500 grams of ration meat and 500 grams of bread per day, it was impossible to transport sufficient supplies for a long campaign, and the army was expected to supplement its rations with what could be taken from the occupied territory.

A re-enactment of an 18th-century market in Quebec. Canadien civilians had very little food as a result of the English siege.

The devastated Church of Notre-Dame de la Victoire, painted by Richard Short in 1761.

remain unmolested on their lands, inhabit their houses and enjoy their religion in security; for these inestimable blessings, I expect the Canadians will take no part in the great contest between the two crowns. But, if in vain obstinacy and misguided valour, they presume to appear in arms, they must expect the most fatal consequences; their habitations destroyed, their sacred temples exposed to an exasperated soldiery, their harvest utterly ruined and the only passage for relief stopped by a most formidable fleet."

When the English troops landed at Île d'Orléans on June 26, most of the inhabitants of the island had already fled, taking refuge in the city. Prior to leaving their homes, the residents had carted off their belongings and concealed them in the surrounding forests, but to no avail. John Knox's journal is full of references such as: "the soldiers brought in great quantities of plunder, such as apparel, kitchen and household furniture, etc. that they found concealed in pits in the wood." Various diaries make continued references to soldiers returning from scouting expeditions loaded with booty and driving livestock into the English camps.

Notwithstanding the looting that was taking place, which was not only condoned by Wolfe but regulated to ensure that all soldiers shared equally in the livestock and goods seized, Wolfe was concerned that the inhabitants themselves remained unharmed in the hopes that they would stay neutral in the conflict. He thus issued the following manifesto to the inhabitants on June 28:

"The King of Great Britain wages no war with the industrious peasant, the sacred orders of religion, or the defenceless women and children; to these, in their distressful circumstances, his royal clemency offers protection. The people may

On the very morning that Wolfe issued his proclamation, a body of English light infantry took refuge from some Canadien and Native skirmishers in a large house. The enemy disappeared but the troops heard voices near the house. They searched the house thoroughly and then left, torching it on their way out. They were appalled to hear the screams of women and children who had concealed themselves in the cellar, and in spite of the attempts by the English to rescue them, the civilians perished in the flames.

Elsewhere, patrols of English soldiers were deliberately destroying buildings against orders but out of sight of senior officers. Again Wolfe issued orders to try to prevent this war on civilians: "No churches, houses or buildings of any kind are to be burned or destroyed without orders: the persons that remain in their habitations, their women and children, are to be treated with humanity; if any violence is offered to a woman, the offender shall be punished with death." In spite of these orders, habitant prisoners and booty continued to be brought into camp. Often, these civilians were captured following ambushes of English soldiers by Canadien militia, were deemed to have refused to remain neutral, and were therefore detained. Wolfe's senior officers treated these prisoners with dignity, and in more than one case entertained the

The English forces landing at Quebec prior to the Battle of the Plains of Abraham, painted circa 1761.

upper-class captives with fine food and wine before they were sent off to be imprisoned on one of the troopships in the river. In one case, a raid by Guy Carleton on Pointe-aux-Trembles resulted in the capture of provisions, livestock, military supplies and 150 women who were well-to-do refugees from the city. Wolfe entertained these "guests" in his camp, and then had them rowed under a flag of truce back to the city. Indigent prisoners, on the other hand, were immediately interned aboard the ships.

There were still atrocities committed by both sides during the guerilla-type warfare that typified the summer of 1759. The American rangers, many of whom had lost friends and families in the border raids of previous years and in the massacres of Fort William Henry or Oswego, were more vengeful and certainly more callous than the English soldiers. At one point Captain Stark's rangers murdered two infants that they had captured. Stark claimed that they had to be killed as their loud crying was giving away the rangers' position while they were being pursued by the enemy. Colonel Fraser of the 78th Highlanders expressed the views of many fellow regular army officers: "I believe this barbarous action proceeded from cow-

ardice and barbarity which seems so natural to a native of America."

Wolfe's attempts to induce the Canadiens to remain neutral failed. A Canadien prisoner taken in arms in July explained the reasons. He said that "he wished the affair was well over, one way or the other; that his countrymen were all discontented, and would either surrender, or disperse and act a neutral part, if it was not for the persuasions of their priests and the fear of being maltreated by the savages, with whom they are threatened on all occasions." Montcalm had also threatened the Canadiens, saying that the Native allies would treat any neutral inhabitant as an enemy.

On learning that his leniency was not producing the expected result of keeping the Canadiens neutral, and perhaps to induce the French army to leave the fort to attack his army, Wolfe issued orders that proved tragic for the people of the St. Lawrence Valley. "Our out parties are ordered to burn and lay waste the country for the future, sparing only churches or houses dedicated to divine worship; it is again repeated that women and children are not to be molested on any account whatsoever."

As the villages and farms went up in flames, more civilian prisoners were brought into Wolfe's camp. While the rangers treated their captives roughly, the common English soldiers felt compassion for the common folk. Colonel Fraser, who was present throughout the campaign, wrote: "Though these acts of hostility may be warrantable by the law and rules of war, yet, as humanity is far from being incompatible with the character of a soldier, any man who is possessed of the least share of it cannot help sympathizing with, and being sincerely affected at the miseries of his fellow creatures, though even his enemies…." Many of these captives had been hiding in the woods for days and were dirty, dishevelled and starving. English soldiers shared their own meager rations, blankets and tobacco with their prisoners before sending them off to the troopships to join the other captives.

The people suffered and the city was being slowly destroyed, but still the French flag flew defiantly over the walls of Quebec.

The Plains of Abraham

By the beginning of September, Wolfe had to make a decision. Niagara had fallen, preventing French reinforcements from reaching Quebec from the west. Amherst was stalled on Lake Champlain and Wolfe could expect no additional troops from that direction. His own army was growing restless and autumn was approaching. Soon the large supporting fleet would have to leave the St. Lawrence before freeze-up. Wolfe would have to either attack the seemingly impregnable Quebec fortifications or call off the campaign. The city had been heavily damaged by the long English bombardment, but its ramparts were still manned and the French guns continued to fire back. Wolfe had time for only one desperate assault on the city.

During this time, the English fleet continued to cruise the St. Lawrence between Quebec and Pointe-aux-Trembles, 25 kilometres upriver from the city. French forces under Louis-Antoine de Bougainville had to continually move from Pointe-aux-Trembles to Ste-Foy, a short distance west of Quebec, to foil any attempted landing. During these cruises, the English were able to thoroughly scout the shore for poten-

Charles William Jefferys' dramatic, but not historically accurate, representation of Montcalm leading his troops at the Plains of Abraham.

tial landing spots. Finally, Wolfe planned for an amphibious assault at Pointe-aux-Trembles where all roadways from the west to Quebec joined. This would cut off any French supplies and reinforcements from reaching the city. Montcalm had expected an attack on the Beauport shore to the east, and concentrated many of his troops there.

Just prior to September 13, however, Wolfe learned that a path from the Anse-aux-Foulons, just west of the city, was poorly defended by a small force under the command of Captain Louis du Pont du Chambon de Vergor, the man who had surrendered Fort Beauséjour in 1755.

Wolfe decided to gamble that his army could climb the steep path to the Plains of Abraham and overwhelm the small force guarding it before the French could respond with reinforcements from Ste-Foy or from Quebec itself.

In the pre-dawn hours of September 13, Wolfe's troops, who had rowed upriver beyond the Anse-aux-Foulons, ostensibly heading for Pointe-aux-Trembles, drifted back downriver to land below the Anse-aux-Foulons in what is now called Wolfe's Cove. His men quickly climbed the steep gully leading to the plain above the bank, in spite of being challenged by a French sentry. Legend says that one of the English in the vanguard was able to reassure the sentry by answering him in French and causing enough doubt to allow a larger force to scale the heights before the French realized that the troops were English. Desultory gunfire broke out, but the French still did not realize the extent of the invasion. De Vergor sent a runner back towards the city to warn of the English attack,

Fraser's Highlanders animators. The Highlanders made up a significant portion of Wolfe's force.

thin line of English, the redcoats held their fire. On the English flank, Native allies and provincial rangers sniped at the French as they marched forward, and a fierce fire-fight developed between these men and the Canadien militia and their allied Native warriors. With bayonets glistening in the morning sun, regimental flags flapping in the breeze and the pipers of Fraser's Highlanders playing music to stir the soul, the English army stood firm as Montcalm's regulars advanced. The French militia on either end of the French line fired at long range, creating gaps in the red line that were quickly filled to maintain a solid front. Many of the French militiamen then dropped out of the ranks, taking cover or lying down to reload their muskets. These men were left behind as the French regulars continued to advance. As the French marched forward, skirmishers of the individual English regiments fired at them. When the French force, marching forward at a stately pace, was only 30 or 40 metres

but soon his force was overwhelmed as more English soldiers gained the summit and began to organize into lines. Montcalm, at his headquarters at Beauport, was alerted by the sound of musket fire and quickly began to order his troops to meet the threat, which he still considered to be either a feint attack or a minor skirmish.

Wolfe's army continued to gather on the plain and began to march inland until reaching the road to Ste-Foy, where they began advancing toward Quebec. Soon the white-coated French regulars could be seen gathering between Wolfe's army and the city. More and more French regulars and Canadien militia formed ranks on the plain as Wolfe's thin red line slowly advanced and then halted. Montcalm joined his troops at about 10:00 a.m. and formed the French regulars into three columns while the militia gathered on the flanks. Montcalm hoped that a large army under Bougainville would soon arrive from the west, but he nevertheless decided to attack Wolfe's position immediately, while the English were still off balance and before Wolfe could completely deploy his army or develop a strong defensive position.

As the French regulars slowly advanced toward the

A mid-19th century impression of the Plains of Abraham. Wolfe ordered his men to "double shot," or load two musket balls into their weapons. The resulting volley devastated the French line.

Benjamin West's 1770 portrayal of Wolfe's death. The painting is perhaps the least historically accurate version, but it was a huge hit with the English public when it was unveiled.

from the English, the redcoats were given the order to fire a volley with every soldier firing in unison. The English soldiers had been ordered to double-shot their muskets, or to load two musket balls into the weapons. With an explosion like a clap of thunder, Wolfe's soldiers fired a devastating volley into the French ranks. All were blinded by the thick smoke of gunpowder from the discharge. As the morning breeze cleared the smoke, the English advanced a few paces and fired again. Piles of dead and wounded lay in front of the redcoats. Many of the French militia, not trained in this type of terrifying open-field combat, began to flee back to the city. The French regulars wavered, firing back at the English but with their ordered ranks in disarray. Wolfe was down, fatally wounded. Montcalm, racing back and forth on his horse to try and turn back the panicked militia, was also hit.

Along the English line, the order was given to charge the disorganized French troops. With each regiment screaming its regimental slogans, the redcoats quickly advanced with their bayonets levelled. The men of Fraser's Highlanders fired a volley, threw down their muskets, drew their razor-sharp claymore swords and launched a ferocious highland charge at the retreating French. With blood-curdling Gaelic oaths, the kilted Highlanders raced forward, cutting down the now fleeing enemy as they chased them towards the gates of the city. Sergeant Thompson of Fraser's Highlanders described the charge: "If the French gave themselves up quietly, they had no harm done to them, but Faith! if they tried to outrun a Hielandmun [highland man], they stood but a bad chance, for whash! went the broadsword." On the receiving end of this charge, French soldier Joseph Trahan said that he would "never forget Fraser's Highlanders flying wildly after them, with streaming plaids, bonnets and large swords, like so many infuriated demons…."

The French army was now in full retreat. Wolfe lived long

enough to learn that the French were fleeing the field of battle. Montcalm rode back into the city and was taken to the home of a doctor who could do nothing for the general. Within a few hours, he too was dead.

Wolfe's army could still not enter the well-defended city, and Brigadier-General James Murray, now in command, ordered a halt to the wild charge of his troops

An 18th-century engraving of Montcalm's death. He actually died at a Quebec doctor's home, not on the battlefield as portrayed here.

who were now suffering heavy casualties themselves as they approached the French fortifications. It was at this time that Bougainville was seen advancing from Cap Rouge with a sizeable force. Brigadier-General Townsend, closest to the scene, hastily turned his men about, reordered their ranks and moved his field guns into position to meet this new threat. Bougainville was intimidated by the resolute ranks of the English and withdrew to Sillery to give himself more time to assess the situation. East of the city, those French troops still at Beauport under the command of Vaudreuil marched north and then west to join Bougainville's force and eventually all retreated, leaving Quebec to its fate. It is not known why they did not immediately attack the English army but it may be that they overestimated the strength of the enemy.

Quebec was now cut off, surrounded by the English army. A third of the houses in the town had been destroyed, including many of the public buildings. The cathedral had burned, the bishop's palace was destroyed, and although buildings still stood, their roofs were gone and their walls were crumbling. Food was scarce and the citizens were com-

pletely demoralized. Montcalm was dead and the next senior French commanders had retreated with the remnants of the army. The town held out for a few days while the civic leaders debated their next course of action. Meanwhile, the English army on the plains before the city were digging entrenchments and siege works and hauling heavy cannons to begin a new bombardment of Quebec. When the leading citizens of the city, led now by Major Jean-Baptiste-Nicholas-Roch de Ramezy, realized that the French army, now under the command of de Lévis and Vaudreuil, would not return to drive off the English, Quebec was surrendered. The terms of the capitulation were very generous. The surrender document stated that the inhabitants of the city would "be preserved in the possession of their houses, goods, effects, and privileges" and that "the effects of absent officers and inhabitants shall not be touched." Further, the English promised to send guards to ensure that the army would not sack public buildings when they finally entered. English troops marched into the capital on September 18. Quebec was taken, but could it be held?

7

The Capitulation — 1760

"Take upon you the administration of the whole, governing the same if necessary according to the military laws…. I should choose that the inhabitants, whenever any differences arise between them, were suffered to settle them among themselves agreeable to their own laws and customs."
— *Amherst's instructions to Governor James Murray following the Capitulation, September, 1760.*

Following the surrender of Quebec, the largest portion of the English army, the highest-ranking officers among them, prepared to board the ships of the Royal Navy and leave. There was not enough food to sustain the entire army in addition to the civilians of the captured city. Brigadier-General James Murray was left in command of 7,000 men who had survived the battle unwounded. Outside the city, there were still more than that number of active French forces who had retreated in the direction of Montreal where, presumably, they would go into winter quarters. There was also a sizeable number of French regulars and Canadien militia still within the walls of the city. Murray ordered the French regulars to board the English ships still at Quebec to be shipped back to France. The Canadien militiamen were simply sent home after they willingly gave their oaths of allegiance to King George.

A 1770 painting of James Murray, who showed great leniency to the people of Quebec after assuming control of the city.

The Bitter Winter

The English were extremely lenient with the beaten foe. French civic officers were permitted to keep their posts, the people could continue to practise their Roman Catholic religion, the civil laws were maintained, and the French language was not banned. These concessions by the English differed greatly from their approach to the conquest of Scotland in 1746, when not only the Gaelic language but also symbols of Scotland such as the kilt and the bagpipe were proscribed. Similarly in Ireland, the Catholic religion had been banned and a person could be hung for speaking anything other than English. In Quebec, this leniency was necessary to prevent a revolt that could overthrow Murray's small army of occupation. The English hold was tenuous at best and the people were to be treated with kindness and respect to keep them passive, if not supportive.

On October 18, 1759, Saunders' fleet weighed anchor and sailed down the river ahead of the approaching winter. Murray's remaining force had a most daunting task ahead of it before it could expect relief in the spring. The French Commissary-General, Bernier, described the state of the city: "Quebec is nothing but a shapeless mass of ruins. Confusion, disorder, pillage reign even among the inhabitants, for the English make examples of severity every

Another Richard Short painting of the devastation of Quebec. It was difficult to find shelter for civilians and soldiers during the winter of 1760 as a result of the English bombardment the previous year.

John Knox, who kept a journal, spoke to one young soldier who worked tirelessly helping a farmer with his harvest and who refused to accept anything for his labours. When asked why he did not take a share of the harvest the soldier replied that "it would be rank murder to take anything from the poor devils, for they have lost enough already." The soldiers had their rations of hard, dry and weevil-infested ship's biscuit, rancid butter, hard cheese stored in barrels, and salt beef and pork stored in casks of brine. They purchased dried peas locally. No fresh fruit or fresh vegetables were included in the ration, and this led to scurvy outbreaks. The civilians had to rely on handouts from the army or produce from the autumn harvest when they could afford to buy it. Civilians were allowed to leave the city to take refuge with rural relatives while farmers were permitted to bring provisions into the city to sell to the highest bidder. Money was in short supply and the inhabitants would not accept letters of credit from Governor Murray, who finally borrowed money from his soldiers to purchase some fresh food for them.

The winter of 1759 was bitter. It was extremely cold, and with the buildings having been shattered in the bombardment, shelter was inadequate to keep the frost out. Firewood was scarce and the soldiers burned fences and scrap lumber not being used to repair buildings in the town. They also had to cut wood in the countryside, an extremely dangerous undertaking with French Native allies patrolling close to the city, ready to ambush wood-cutting parties that ventured into the surrounding forests.

The English soldiers were not provided with adequate winter uniforms. Their shoes, woollen stockings, woollen

day. Everybody rushes hither and thither, without knowing why. Each searches for his possessions, and, not finding his own, seizes those of other people. English and French, all is chaos alike. The inhabitants, famished and destitute, escape to the country." Murray soon put things straight, establishing order, hanging looters and preparing for the harsh winter ahead.

With much of Quebec in ruins, shelter had to be found for the soldiers, firewood had to be gathered against a frigid Canadian winter, and scant supplies of food had to be stored and securely guarded to be rationed with care until the spring. Above all, Murray had to ensure security by arranging for patrols to continually comb the countryside to prevent surprise attacks by the remaining French army and their Native allies. He also had to take considerable pains to keep the populace of the city docile. His soldiers helped find shelter for civilians bombed out of their houses, assisted the civil authorities to maintain law and order and worked to find sufficient food for the people of Quebec. Although their own supplies were short, the English soldiers shared their rations with the Canadiens, helped with the harvest in October and helped the townsfolk repair their shattered houses. Captain breeches and lined woollen coats proved too heavy in the heat of a North American summer and totally inadequate for a typical Canadian winter. Greatcoats or overcoats were only issued to sentries and were shared within the regiment. Soldiers were issued blankets, but these proved ineffective in protecting them from the frost. They resorted to using carpets, spare pieces of cloth and fur rugs to keep warm. Knox wrote that "our guards on the grand parade make a most grotesque appearance in their different dresses; and our inventions to guard us against the extreme rigor of this climate are various beyond imagination. The uniformity as well as nicety of the clean, methodical soldier is buried in the rough, fur-wrought garb of the frozen Laplander; and we rather resemble a masquerade than a body of regular troops…." In spite of these precautions, many soldiers lost digits to frostbite and in severe cases, gangrene set in, resulting in amputations and death.

A Canadien priest. Citizens of New France were allowed to continue practicing Roman Catholicism in order to keep them from rising up against the small English occupation force.

The brutal winter and shortage of fresh supplies took its toll. Exposure to the elements, scurvy, dysentery and other diseases reduced the ranks. At the Battle of the Plains of Abraham, 616 English soldiers had been killed or wounded. During the winter,

An English Corps of Engineers officer.

672 died of cold and disease while 2,312 were too sick to stand sentry. The sick and wounded, be they French or English, were all cared for in the Quebec General Hospital, where nuns of that institution and of the Hôtel-Dieu under Mother Sainte-Claude saved many lives.

Winter Warfare

In addition to the garrison behind Quebec's walls, Murray sent detachments to establish fortified posts at Ste-Foy, Petit Lorette and Point Lévi. Throughout the winter, the Chevalier de Lévis received intelligence reports of the deteriorating situation while Murray also had spies in the French camp. As the winter progressed, de Lévis started to push larger parties toward Quebec and established several bases. In February, on learning of one such French stronghold near St. Augustin, within striking distance of Quebec, Murray sent an army of 500 men to attack them. After a brisk firefight, the French retreated, and the English pressed on quickly enough to capture 80 French soldiers. The English soldiers became very adept at fighting the French and their Native allies in several small actions in the forests surrounding Quebec, but the cold and privations of winter continued to pare down the number of effective soldiers available to Murray. By the spring, only half his original garrison was considered fit for duty.

Elsewhere, the Seven Years War had been going well for the English and their Prussian allies against France. In India, a decisive victory at Wandiwash ensured that the English would retain a firm hold on the southern half of India, and by January of 1760, the French were all but expelled from the entire continent. On August 1, 1759, the Prussians and

English had soundly beaten a French army at the Battle of Minden, thus saving Hanover from a French invasion. On the high seas, the Royal Navy triumphed, winning a major sea battle at Quiberon Bay off the coast of France in August. This crucial battle crippled the French Atlantic fleet, making the Royal Navy the undisputed ruler of the Atlantic.

In England, William Pitt received reports of Quebec's capture and the government ordered celebrations of thanksgiving to be held in London to celebrate Wolfe's victory. Pitt now decided to administer the coup de grace to the French presence in North America and ordered an all-out effort against Canada to begin in the late spring. The strategy was simple. Jeffery Amherst, who remained in America as the commander-in-chief on the continent, was sent orders to destroy the remnant of the French army holding out at Montreal. Amherst developed plans to advance against Montreal on three fronts, from the Lake Champlain area, from Quebec and from Oswego.

Canadien militia in winter dress. The French troops were better able to adapt to the bitter winter of 1760 than their English counterparts, whose uniforms were inadequate.

The Decision to Attack Quebec

Chevalier de Lévis, now commander-in-chief, and Governor Vaudreuil were at Montreal with the bulk of the French army, a body of men that was in considerably larger numbers than Murray's command at Quebec. They realized, of course, that the English now controlled Quebec and the St. Lawrence, Oswego and Lake Ontario and that they had a stronghold on Lake Champlain with only the small fort at Île-aux-Noix standing between the English and the invasion route to Montreal. With the exception of the small detachments sent to harass the English near Quebec, de Lévis concentrated his men in barracks behind the inadequate defences at Montreal and prepared plans for delaying the inevitable English assault

on that city. Captain Pierre Pouchot, the man who had held Niagara against heavy odds in 1759, was ordered to take 300 men and build a fort on Île Royale at the head of a treacherous set of rapids in the St. Lawrence near Oswegatchie, just downriver from present-day Prescott, Ontario. Chevalier de Bougainville at Île-aux-Noix was ordered to block the Lake Champlain route as long as possible against an expected English advance to the St. Lawrence from that direction. De Lévis prepared dispatches to France asking for food, supplies, heavy artillery and more soldiers. This plea for help had been sent out before the river froze in December, in a small ship that was able to evade the English fleets that plied the Atlantic and kept a close watch on French ports.

General de Lévis realized that Montreal was a difficult spot to defend. There were too many approaches to the city and its weak defences could not withstand a long siege. This city contained as many 7,000 inhabitants, concentrated below the mountain (now known as Old Montreal). The main town was surrounded by a low stone wall with a wooden palisade and a shallow ditch. The fortifications could not withstand an attack by a well-equipped army, and the artillery was insufficient to fend off a determined attack. Montreal was not considered to be a military strongpoint but a commercial hub — the jumping-off point into the interior of the continent, tuned more to trade than war. Thanks to his spies in and around Quebec, de Lévis was very aware of the weakness of Murray's force there. General de Lévis and Governor Vaudreuil realized that the key to saving New France, if that was still possible, was to retake Quebec and hold it until French reinforcements could arrive in the late spring. To be successful, they would have to act before the English garrison of Quebec could be reinforced as it undoubtedly would bc as soon as the St. Lawrence River was ice-free and navigable.

Vaudreuil and de Lévis both believed that Canada would not be totally abandoned by France and that some relief would come in the spring. They felt that as long as they could hold on, preferably behind the fortifications of Quebec, Canada could be kept in French hands until ongoing treaty negotiations in Europe would return captured property to France. They realized that France had not been forthcoming with support in the past two years, but felt that the situation now demanded action. In Europe, however, and on the oceans, France was in dire straits and could afford to send very little relief. Ignorant of the real situation overseas, de Lévis envisioned his stalwart little band of regulars, assisted once again by the inhabitants and the Native nations, recapturing Quebec and receiving the required aid.

Compagnies franches de la Marine re-enactors in Montreal in 2002.

The Habitants

The people of the St. Lawrence valley had suffered through five years of hostilities that had taken a heavy toll on the population and the economy. With the exception of Trois-Riviéres, Montreal and Quebec, New France was an agrarian society. Most Canadiens lived through subsistence farming, growing enough crops and raising enough livestock to feed their families. This was supplemented through fishing and hunting in season. Very little surplus was produced.

In the cities, there were merchants and small craftsmen, but even the latter had to eke out their living through tending gardens and keeping livestock.

While the English parliament had made the capture of Canada a priority after 1757, the government of France placed far less importance on the North American phase of the Seven Years War. Therefore, the number of English regulars committed to the conquest of New France was considerably larger than the French regular army defending the colony. As each year went by, increasing numbers of Canadiens had been called up for service. Many had been killed, wounded or sickened and the farms had suffered severely, with the men unable to tend them as well as they should. While production decreased, the demand for grain and meat increased to feed the men on campaign and the Native allies and their families. By 1760, there were shortages in the richest of agricultural areas as well as in the cities. For the Canadiens, the war could not be sustained.

With the capture of Quebec, many Canadiens in the area of English control, once they realized that the English would not oppress them but allow them to pursue their livelihoods, undoubtedly breathed a sigh of relief. For those in the areas not controlled by the English, it was difficult to decide on a course of action. De Lévis had made it clear that the Canadiens would be expected to fill their role as militia and that neutrality was not an option. Those who would remain neutral would be considered to be enemies of New France. Those Native allies who remained active threatened the Canadiens who would not actively support the dying French cause. When General de Lévis called again on the militia for his intended attack on Quebec, the men responded as required but with little enthusiasm.

The Second Battle of the Plains of Abraham

Leaving only a small force at Montreal to guard government stores, de Lévis left with his army of 7,000 men on April 20, 1760, to attack Quebec. This was a formidable army of battle-hardened regulars and Canadien militia. De Lévis had assembled as much ammunition, supplies and artillery as he

A 19th-century engraving of the Battle of Ste-Foy, in which more soldiers died than on the Plains of Abraham.

could gather and transport. The artillery left something to be desired as the 12 small cannons hauled along would be valuable in an open field battle against infantry forces but not effective against strong fortifications. The French did not have the heavy guns required to break down the walls of the fortification to allow a direct assault on Quebec. It is difficult to determine what de Lévis hoped for in attacking the city at this time. He had enough men to bottle the English up inside and hopefully starve them into surrendering, but that was all. Perhaps de Lévis felt that he would be able to sustain a siege until French reinforcements arrived by ship in the spring and, with their heavy guns, would facilitate the recapture of the city. Although an open battle on the fields outside Quebec was less desirable as such actions normally caused heavy casualties, this possibility had the potential of deciding the issue quickly, particularly if the populace of Quebec rose up at the same time against the English garrison. Regardless of de Lévis' strategy in attacking Quebec, it was clear that the French had to capture it before an English relief force could arrive.

Just as the French had spies in the English camp, the English received intelligence outlining the French movements. Among others, Murray employed a French merchant as an agent. This man seemed able to miraculously slip supplies out of Quebec to bring to Montreal and was highly regarded by the French leadership for his acumen in moving goods right under the noses of the English. In fact, he sent messages back to Murray informing him of French plans and strategies. Murray also received reports from French deserters who occasionally turned themselves in to English patrols and from inhabitants who tried to ingratiate themselves with the English. Therefore, Murray was forewarned of the pending French attack.

The French troops travelled down the St. Lawrence in dozens of batteaux escorted by two frigates. On April 24, de Lévis's army reached Pointe-aux-Trembles, where they disembarked to march inland. Three days later, his advance troops approached Ste-Foy, only 10 kilometres from Quebec, and prepared to attack.

The winter of 1759–60 had been a difficult one for Brigadier-General James Murray and his troops, many of whom still languished in makeshift hospitals, victims of poor food and cruel weather. When scouts brought word of the French advance, Murray rallied 3,800 men and marched them towards Ste-Foy, where simple defence works of trenches and abatis had been prepared. As de Lévis finally arrived with his main force, the French troops began to outflank the English. Murray discovered the French manoeuvre and withdrew his men back towards Quebec where they took a stand on the Plains of Abraham, near the spot where Montcalm's troops had formed on September 13 of the previous year.

General de Lévis had hoped to avoid a large open battle with the English, but seeing them drawn up in their ranks, and realizing that his own force outnumbered them, he ordered the attack. The battered flags of the regular regiments were unfurled, the drummers beat the "pas-de-charge" on their frozen drums, and the French army advanced across the plain to approach within musket range of the English. Part of the French army was still on the road from Pointe-aux-Trembles and de Lévis realized that his force would be continually reinforced as the battle raged. At the beginning of this battle of Ste-Foy on the morning of April 27, however, both armies were similar in size.

In classically fought battles in this era, opponents faced each other with their soldiers spread out in long parallel lines across the field. These closely packed ranks would then fire volleys in unison with individual companies or battalions firing as a group. One of the belligerents could gain an advantage on the enemy if they could "outflank" them by marching a group of soldiers so they were perpendicular to the enemy line. That way, a mass of muskets could be brought to bear against the width of the thin line rather than against the breadth. This allowed the attackers to "turn the flank" — or attack the side rather than the front of the enemy line — and in so doing, to break down the enemy order and cause the troops to panic.

As the French were taking position, Murray noticed that the left side of the enemy army was in some disarray and decided that he could turn that flank by quickly attacking. His men set forth but got bogged down in deep snow and mud, allowing the French, in turn, to threaten the English flanks. A very hot fight ensued, with both armies manoeuvring in an attempt to outflank the other. Murray feared that the French were gaining on his force. Casualties very rapidly mounted and Murray became aware that more French forces were on their way to the battlefield. He ordered a retreat and his men withdrew in a less than orderly fashion back from the field and into the fortifications of Quebec, abandoning a few bogged-down cannons on the field. The Battle of Ste-Foy, or second Battle of the Plains of Abraham, was over. The action had been extremely bloody for both armies, causing more casualties than had the original Battle of the Plains of Abraham. At the Battle of Ste-Foy, the French had 193 men killed and 640 wounded while the English suffered losses of 259 dead and 829 wounded. On the day that Wolfe and Montcalm were killed at the first battle, the English had 58 killed and 558 wounded while the French had twice as many killed and similar numbers of wounded.

The French could not assault the fort without heavy artillery and fell back on one of de Lévis' original plans to lay siege to Quebec to prevent soldiers from leaving the city or food from getting through to it. Then they would await reinforcements from France to help retake the city. Trenches started by the English in September were expanded and new ones were dug. Protected emplacements for the French guns and for a few English cannons captured during the battle were also constructed. On May 11, 1760, the French began bombarding Quebec, more to harass the English than to destroy the defences, although they did cause severe damage to one of the bastions of the main fortifications.

Meanwhile, a small convoy of five transports carrying guns, food, ammunition and 400 troops had set out from France in response to de Lévis' earlier requests for aid. The French navy could afford only one escorting ship, the frigate *Machault*. The convoy was chased by ships of the Royal Navy under the command of Admiral Boscawen and three of the transports were captured. The *Machault* and the surviving transports took shelter in Chaleur Bay where the Restigouche River empties into the St. Lawrence. Sailors ferried the ship's cannons to shore, where batteries were constructed to guard the vessels, now hemmed in by the English fleet. This stalemate continued until July, when the French finally burned their ships to prevent their capture.

At Quebec, both French and English realized that the city would likely fall if French ships arrived first on the scene. If an English ship arrived first, it would mean that Quebec would be re-supplied and therefore would continue to be held by the English. Both sides, the English behind the city's fortifications, and the French in their entrenchments, anxiously watched as the ice on the river began to break up in rising spring temperatures. Officers of both armies trained telescopes downriver for the first site of a sail. Finally, on May 16, a ship could be seen approaching the town, but it was flying no flags so it was impossible to tell whether it was French or English. Murray ordered a large English flag to be raised from the ramparts of Quebec and the ship followed suit, the grand union breaking open from the mainmast and fluttering in the breeze. The ship was the frigate *Lowestoff*, vanguard of a larger English fleet bringing more troops, supplies and food for the beleaguered garrison of Quebec. John Knox described the elation of the troops in the besieged city: "The gladness of the troops is not to be expressed; both officers and soldiers mounted the parapets in the face of the enemy, and huzzaed, with their hats in the air, for almost an hour; the garrison, the enemy's camp, the bay and the adjacent country for several miles, resounded with our shouts and the thunder of our artillery; for the Gunners were so elated, that they did nothing but fire load and fire for a considerable time…."

De Lévis had no choice but to lift the siege and march his troops back to Montreal to prepare to meet Amherst's expected attack down the St. Lawrence. Quebec was now firmly in English hands, with any hopes by the French of recapturing the city completely dashed. Those few Natives still allied with the French certainly recognized the hopelessness of the situation and many met with the English to declare their neutrality or to actually offer military assistance in the final defeat of New France. With the threat of Native reprisals lifted, many Canadiens felt secure in deserting the army and submitting to the English juggernaut.

A French commemorative medal featuring King Louis XV.

Murray's Advance to Montreal

The English commander-in-chief, General Jeffery Amherst,

A late 18th-century portrait of Sir Jeffery Amherst, who led the final assault on the French at Montreal.

planned the final assault on the French in Canada as a three-part movement. Murray would go upriver from Quebec, Brigadier-General William Haviland would advance up the Lake Champlain-Richelieu River route, and Amherst himself would lead an army from Oswego down the St. Lawrence River.

The three armies would converge on Montreal, cutting off any escaping French forces and capturing the remnant of their army there.

On July 13, 1760, General Murray set off from Quebec with 2,200 men. Most were embarked on 32 armed vessels, 9 gunboats and a fleet of batteaux, but others marched by land. On the slow journey upriver to Montreal, his flotilla was harassed at times by small pockets of French soldiers on shore, but this did little to delay his advance. What did slow him down were the hordes of French Canadiens who would enter his camps at each stop along the river to proclaim their neutrality and swear loyalty to King George III. The Canadiens, seeing this final advance on the remnant of the French army, realized that the war was nearing its end and wished to prove their neutrality in an attempt to save their farms.

Finally, on August 27, Murray's flotilla dropped anchor just downriver from Montreal. Troops were landed and were joined by those who had marched by land. His army quickly captured the south shore opposite Montreal but did not press the attack on the Island of Montreal itself. Rather, the soldiers dug trenches, sited cannons and built defensive positions behind which they would wait for the approach of Amherst's other two armies.

The Fall of Île-aux-Noix

During the winter of 1759–60 the English had been busy building ships and batteaux on Lake Champlain to use in the coming campaign against Île-aux-Noix. The island on the Richelieu was fortified and protected by chains slung across the river and by two small armed vessels. The garrison, under the command of Bougainville, consisted of 1,450 infantrymen and a small group of artillerymen to tend the few cannons at the fort.

On August 11, Haviland launched his campaign up the Richelieu after a long summer of mustering provincials, equipping and outfitting the men, and hauling supplies past Albany to the jumping-off position at Crown Point. His army totalled around 3,500 men. By August 19, the English had reached the vicinity of Île-aux-Noix, hastily hauled cannons to shore and begun bombarding the fort. It was too risky to attempt an amphibious assault while the French naval vessels sailed the river, but on August 25 English raiders captured both boats. The way was now open for an assault on the island. Bougainville knew that it would be fruitless to try and stop Haviland's army. He had few Native allies with him, and the type of ambush that had stopped Braddock five years earlier could not be contemplated without these experienced forest fighters.

On the night of August 27, Bougainville's small force evacuated its position at Île-aux-Noix and retreated towards Montreal. As the small French army passed Fort St-Jean and Fort Chambly, Bougainville withdrew the garrisons of these lightly manned posts and burned the fort buildings. The way was now clear for the second wave of the English advance on Montreal. Haviland's army arrived near the city on September 5, linking up with Murray's force.

An English medal awarded to Native allies who accompanied Amherst's army to Montreal.

au Baril (modern day Maitland, Ontario) and Oswegatchie or Fort La Presentation (Ogdensburg, New York). The last leg of his journey required passage through several treacherous sets of rapids that made river travel dangerous between Oswegatchie and Montreal. But first, the English had to get by the defences manned by a small body of French troops under the command of the tenacious Pierre Pouchot. Pierre Pouchot had been paroled and exchanged following the surrender of Fort Niagara the previous year and had returned to the Chevalier de Lévis's remnant army. De Lévis had sent Pouchot up the St. Lawrence to construct a small fort to delay Amherst's advance. Pouchot set his garrison of 300 men to work fortifying Île Royale, a small island in the middle of the St. Lawrence at the head of the first set of rapids in the river. His men built shelters, raised earthworks, dug a moat, filled it with water from the river and hauled trees from the mainland to surround the fort with abatis. The new fort was christened Fort de Lévis.

The French had no heavy cannons at Fort de Lévis with which to damage the English flotilla. Pouchot sent men to the

Fort de Lévis — the Last Stand

General Amherst set off from Albany with a huge army of more than 14,000 men — regulars, provincials and Native allies. They advanced up the Mohawk River, across the Great Carrying Place and down the Oswego River. Leaving a strong garrison at Oswego they embarked in long boats and batteaux, escorted by the sloops of war, *Onondaga* and *Mohawk*, and sailed to the St. Lawrence River to begin the descent on Montreal. On August 16, his flotilla had passed the Thousand Islands of the St. Lawrence River and reached the area of modern-day Prescott, Ontario. His troops overran the small French shipyard of Pointe

Fort Chambly, 2002. De Lévis burned this fort before surrendering Montreal to the English.

ruins of Fort Frontenac to salvage French guns that had been rendered unserviceable during the capture of Frontenac by Bradstreet two years earlier. The English had partially smashed the guns so they would not fit on gun carriages, so Pouchot had the gun barrels lashed to logs and placed on the shore of Île Royale where they could fire low shots at approaching English vessels.

When Amherst's army arrived on the scene, the English general was quick to assess the danger imposed by the fort. He swung into action, moved heavy artillery to the northern shore (near modern-day Johnstown) and opened fire on Fort de Lévis. For more than a week, heavy cannons and mortars bombarded the French island, rendering Pouchot's makeshift gun batteries useless. Finally, on August 26, English grenadiers and highlanders, stripped down to breeches and shirts to move quickly in the attack, approached the island in a group of batteaux and quickly swarmed over Fort de Lévis' battered defences. Pouchot surrendered his small garrison as the grenadiers burst into the redoubt.

Amherst gathered his army back together, reloaded his cannons and mortars onto his barges and prepared to set off on the final leg of the journey to Montreal. He renamed Fort de Lévis Fort William Augustus, left a small garrison to staff it, and sailed down the rapids of the St. Lawrence River. The trip was a deadly one for many. In spite of being guided through the white water by experienced Mohawk rivermen, several batteaux were lost in the churning rapids. Over 80 men drowned on the way down to Montreal. On September 6, Amherst finally reached his destination, landing on the west end of Montreal Island.

Montreal

In the past century, the city of Montreal had evolved into a very active commercial centre. The fur trade empire was based there and loads of furs from the interior arrived at Montreal down the St. Lawrence or Ottawa rivers. It was from here that troops assembled on the routes to the interior posts. However, it was not a fortress as Quebec had been.

As the inhabitants watched the English armies converge on the city, they prayed that the proud French regulars under de Lévis would not resist. Montreal's defences were not meant to keep out a well-equipped European army, but were built as low stone walls, light earthworks and palisades to protect the main town from any attack by Native war parties. Any defence of this inadequate position would be suicide. Thankfully, Governor Vaudreuil and General de Lévis had come to the same conclusion and would not be given to heroics.

The French army under de Lévis' command, now reduced to 2,100 regulars, a small force of militiamen under the command of Vaudreuil and a contingent of Native warriors under their own leaders were now surrounded by an overwhelming English force. There was no escape route open and nowhere to go if there were. All was lost. On September 7, de Lévis' lieutenant, Bougainville, approached Amherst under a red flag of truce to arrange an end to hostilities, asking for terms that would allow the proud regulars to march out of Montreal with the honours of war — arms carried and drums beating. Amherst initially refused, insisting on an unconditional surrender, but finally worked out an agreement that was extremely lenient in its treatment of the French. The next day, Vaudreuil and Amherst signed the articles of capitulation. The formal surrender of the French, not only of Montreal but also of New France, was to take place on the following day. That night the French regulars burned their flags, not wanting to suffer the indignity of seeing them captured by the English. On the morning of September 9, the French regulars marched out of the weak fortifications of Montreal and formed up outside of the walls, awaiting their fate. New France had capitulated.

The Articles of Capitulation

The terms of the capitulation of Montreal were similar to those of Quebec a year before and were to set the character of Quebec under English rule. Throughout the document, Vaudreuil had ensured that his own personal property and goods would not be adversely affected and he even stipulated the type of accommodations he would require on board the English ship that would return him to France. The English also agreed that the regular soldiers and anyone else in New France who wished it would be shipped back to France. Those who chose to stay would have to swear an oath of allegiance to King George. Militia and Native allies were

A 20th-century impression of English troops entering Montreal. The city lacked armed fortifications and was a difficult spot for the French to defend.

permitted to return to their homes "unmolested" and were not taken to account for their actions during the war. All were pardoned. Oddly, while everyone else could return to their homes, this concession was not granted to the exiled Acadians. Vaudreuil had requested this but Amherst refused to comply. It was still felt that the Acadians had been a special case because they were inhabitants of English territory and had refused to swear unconditional allegiance to the king. The most important section of the document confirmed that the Canadiens would be permitted to keep their language, their properties, their civil law, and their religion. Roman Catholicism, proscribed elsewhere in the British Empire, was permitted to flourish in Canada. Finally, the document stated that Canadiens would have the same rights in commerce and trade as their fellow British subjects. For Canada, it was to be business as usual but under a different flag. Many inhabitants

assumed that Canada would again return to France when the Seven Years War finally ground to a halt.

With the capitulation at Montreal, the French and Indian War was over. Elsewhere in the world, the Seven Years War would continue for another two and half years. While the English and French were now at peace in North America, other issues remained unresolved, particularly among Native people, who had suffered incredibly during the conflict. They had not been conquered and had lost no major battles, but with the end of the French regime in Canada, the Native nations found themselves thrust out of the role that they had long enjoyed: holding the balance of power in conflicts between the European colonists. In the next few years, many of the Native nations of the east were to make their own bid for control of North America.

8

THE ROAD TO REVOLUTION — 1760–1763

With the capitulation of New France at Montreal, the French had finally been defeated after more than a century of conflict in North America. The peace was precarious, however, leaving many issues unresolved. In past conflicts between the English and French, the peace treaties ending the wars had returned captured territory. Louisbourg, for example, had been captured in 1745 only to be returned to France at the end of the war. Many in Canada thought that the treaty that would eventually end the Seven Years War would result in the return of Canada to the King of France. They were mistaken. The rich harvest of furs that had made New France a valuable colony had been replaced in global economic value by sugar, spice and tobacco. France was more interested in maintaining its trade networks with the West Indies and Asia than in the bounties of the American wilderness. In the newly conquered territory of Canada, the Canadiens would begin a long struggle to retain their language and culture.

Among the Native nations of eastern

A View of the Cathedral, Jesuits College, and Recollet Friars Church, taken from the Gate of the Governor's House, 1761, *by Richard Short.*

North America, the struggle for survival became more serious as land speculators and settlers turned covetous eyes on Native-controlled territories in the interior of the continent. In the English colonies, which had ultimately worked together to play a major role in the expulsion of the French, men began to assert their own rights more fervently, questioning the system of government whereby the colonies were controlled by a parliament in England in which they had no direct representation.

The conquest of Canada had repercussions throughout the continent. The people of New France no longer played a key role in maintaining the French empire in America and now had to struggle to develop new relationships with the English conquerors. Canny Scottish merchants were moving in to take control of the fur trade and Canadien merchants had to build new networks of partners and supply sources. The people of the English colonies no longer had to rely on the mother country to defend their settlements against French encroachments. They began to think of themselves more as North Americans than as transplanted English, Irish or Scots. Finally, the Native nations found that their English allies, who now had no rivals on the continent, were far less generous with the bestowing of gifts of manufactured goods to maintain their loyalty.

The End of the Seven Years War

On October 25, 1760, George II died and his grandson George III became King of England. The new king was conscious of the depletion of the English treasury in the pursuit of the Seven Years War and began to take steps to end the costly conflict. His friend and mentor, the Earl of Bute, was appointed to join William Pitt as a co-secretary of state, in effect sharing the duties of what would later be called the prime minister. Until then, England had been supplying money to the Prussians to help them continue the war against France, but Bute was able to influence parliament to withdraw this funding. The English had, by this time, more than 25,000 troops in Europe, and that expense alone was deemed to be prohibitive. England wanted peace.

Prussia was being pressed closely by a coalition of France, Austria and Russia, which had allied with various German Catholic princes. The Prussians won minor victories at

Another painting by Charles William Jefferys of Ottawa leader Pontiac threatening Major Henry Gladwyn, the commander of Fort Detroit.

Ziegenhagen and Warburg in 1760, but by the end of the year the French had crossed the Rhine River and controlled German territory across the west of what is now Germany. Throughout the following year, there were numerous skirmishes with the French and their allies making no further territorial conquests while the Prussians were unable to expel them from German soil. It seemed that Prussia would eventually lose the war.

In January 1762, Czarina Elizabeth of Russia died and Peter III became Czar. Peter admired the Prussians and pulled Russia out of the coalition with France and Austria. With Russia no longer a threat, the Prussians were able to strike out at Austria, retaking the Principality of Silesia. They then turned and drove the French from southern Hanover and from Hesse. With Prussia's boundaries now more or less secure, Frederick of Prussia was ready to talk peace.

France had continued to be active on the diplomatic front, and while French commissioners continued to meet with the English to discuss an end to the war, other French agents were secretly negotiating with the Spanish to encourage them to declare war on England. On January 18, 1762, Spain declared war on England. The English, reluctant to act against Spain prior to a declaration of war, now began attacking Spanish colonies.

On June 6, 1762, a large English fleet carrying more than 14,000 soldiers under the command of General the Earl of Abermarle arrived off the Spanish colony of Cuba, intent on capturing the port of Havana, which was the most important Spanish possession in the Caribbean. Following a terrific bombardment, Havana surrendered on August 14. British forces similarly captured Manila in October along with the French colonies of Martinique and Guadeloupe. The French and Spanish fleets were no match for the Royal Navy, which could land invasion forces to attack their colonies with impunity around the globe. All belligerents now wanted peace.

While there were still minor actions in America in 1762, including the French capture of St. John's, Newfoundland, in June and its subsequent recapture by the English in September, it was clear that the war was winding down. Peace talks began in late autumn of 1762 and finally, on February 10, 1763, a peace treaty was ratified in Paris, finally ending the Seven Years War.

The Treaty of Paris shows how much both the

An Algonkian sash. Elaborate, finger-woven sashes were made in Quebec and became very popular items of Native dress.

French and Spanish valued their colonies where sugar plantations flourished and their ports guarded the routes to the spices of Asia and India. France did not argue strongly for the retention of Canada, but pushed for Martinique, Guadeloupe, St. Lucia and Goree. To keep a hand in the very important cod fishery on the Grand Banks off Newfoundland, they negotiated to keep the islands of St-Pierre and Miquelon, still part of France today. Spain recovered Manila and Havana but surrendered Florida to the English. When word of the treaty reached Canada in the spring, many of the Canadiens were shocked. They had assumed that the treaty would restore French Canada to France and that life would proceed as before. Canada, written off by Voltaire as "a few acres of snow," had been abandoned to the traditional English enemy.

The Native Struggle for Sovereignty

In the many long years since the arrival of Europeans in North America, the Native nations of North America had to continually study the political atmosphere and develop alliances and policies best suited to ensure that they would not be swept away by one of the powerful European nations struggling for control of the continent.

The Seven Years War had been a confusing time for the Native nations of eastern North America. At the beginning of the conflict, the French seemed to be winning. They were perceived by Native people to be fair in trade and respectful in their dealings. They seemed to want only to preserve their economic trade empire, not to dispossess the First Nations and settle their land. As the war progressed, the French proved less able to defend their positions and were unable to present sufficient gifts of manufactured goods to Native peoples. Further, while the colonial regular soldiers and officers and the Canadiens themselves treated the Native peoples as equals, welcoming them into their homes and intermarrying with their people, the officers and soldiers from France seemed to treat them with some disdain, regarding their warriors not as allies but as less-valued auxiliary forces. By the end of the struggle, many Natives had a lowered opinion of their former French allies.

The English attitude toward Native peoples was even more confusing. Like their French counterparts, English regular army officers treated the Native leaders poorly, trying to order them on campaign rather than consulting with them. While some of the colonists who lived close to Native neighbours, like Sir William Johnson, treated them with a great deal of friendship and respect, other frontier people feared and detested them, referring to them as savages and, in effect, dehumanizing them in their dealings. Further, the English settlers seemed to feel free to acquire Native lands through fraudulent contracts, and then fill them with settlers. These people then trespassed on traditional hunting grounds, decimating the game on which the Native people depended for survival. The lack of respect would shortly reach a critical point that could have completely changed the character of North America today.

The Reduction of Gifts

Following the final defeat of the French, General Jeffery Amherst immediately began measures to bring his expenses under control. Amherst regarded Natives as uncivilized wards of the state who would be a continuing source of trouble unless they were taught the principles of commerce, and could learn to fend for themselves and not rely on the huge amount of manufactured goods supplied to them by the English government. Although these gifts were important tokens of the Native concept of free sharing among friends, Amherst thought of them not as presents but as payment to auxiliaries during war. With the war over, he ordered his fort commanders to cut back on the gifts given to the various nations. He also ordered them to carefully regulate trade to ensure Native people got a fair return of the manufactured goods in the merchants' warehouses in exchange for their fish, furs and maple sugar. He further banned the trading of rum, because of its negative effects on many Native people. He also limited the amount of shot and gunpowder available to the Native peoples, fearing

Pontiac leading the rebellion against the English in 1763.

that this ammunition could be used in war against the English.

All of this went against the advice of those such as Sir William Johnson, who knew and understood the nature of friendship, the importance of gifts and the danger of treating the proud Native peoples like errant children requiring protection. What Amherst's policies succeeded in doing was to further alienate many of the Natives who had previously allied themselves with the English while reminding those who had fought alongside the French of the golden days under the alliance with the French king.

The Delaware Prophet

From time to time among the nations of North America, a visionary would claim to have received instructions from the "Giver of Life" or "the Creator." These prophets would share their visions with their own village, and word of their prophecies would quickly spread between their nation and others. Toward the end of the war in North America, a new prophet, Neolin of the Delaware, had a vision. He claimed that the Giver of Life had revealed to him the steps that Natives should take to regain their sovereignty and self-respect, thereby creating a paradise in America that would ensure their survival and prosperity. The Delaware Prophet, as he is known to history, spoke at many gatherings. People from other nations travelled great distances to hear his words.

According to Neolin, the Native nations had to shun

European manufactured goods and avoid the whites altogether, associating only with other Natives. They had to return to their old ways of living off the land, wearing tanned skins rather than European cloth, using Native weapons and tools rather than firearms and iron implements, and they should stop the destructive hunting of animals simply for their furs to trade. The prophecy went further. If the Native people embraced this simpler traditional lifestyle and if they all joined together in a common cause, the Giver of Life would force the whites to leave America, returning to their own homes across the ocean.

In the wake of the devastation of the Seven Years War and the subsequent treatment that Natives were receiving from the English conquerors, the words of the Delaware Prophet struck a note that resounded through Native villages. The prophecy would be used by war leaders to encourage young men to take up arms and strike against the English, who were increasingly seen as interlopers and enemies of the Native peoples. The resulting series of small wars against the English came close to wresting control of the interior of North America from them.

An Ottawa pouch and knife with sheath. The decorative work on the pouch and sheath is done with dyed porcupine quills, along with beads and "tinkle cones" of European manufacture. The beads and cones, along with the knife and silver brooches, were typical gifts or trade items.

The 1763 Uprising

In the spring of 1763, the various elements of dissatisfaction came to a head and in several areas warriors from a number of nations made what seemed to be a concerted effort to defeat the English. This series of small actions is collectively and erroneously known as "Pontiac's Conspiracy," named for an influential Ottawa war chief who led attacks by an alliance of several nations against Detroit.

On September 13, 1760, Robert Rogers was sent from Montreal with a force of rangers and soldiers of the 60th Regiment to deliver news of the capitulation to interior posts still held by French forces. The chief of these was Fort Pontchartrain at Detroit. When Rogers arrived to accept the surrender of the fort, the Native people nearby were astounded to see the French flag lowered while the English flag was raised and to see the French soldiers march from the fort, as if on parade, without a shot being fired. To the Ottawa, Wyandot, Pottawatomie and Chippewa people in attendance, the fact that the English did not punish the French, or even disarm them, was peculiar. Further, the French civilian populace treated the English soldiers with dignity and respect and, in turn, the English permitted the inhabitants to go about their daily business undisturbed.

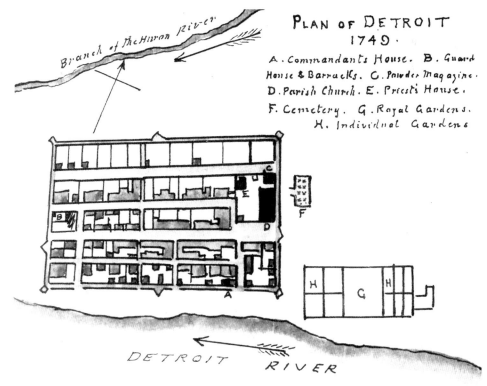

PLAN OF DETROIT
1749.

A. Commandants House. B. Guard House & Barracks. C. Powder Magazine. D. Parish Church. E. Priests House. F. Cemetery. G. Royal Gardens. H. Individual Gardens

A plan of Fort Detroit, drawn in 1749. Ottawa leader Pontiac held the fort under siege for the entire summer of 1763.

In January 1761, the first English trader arrived at Detroit, but when approached by local Natives, he would neither give nor sell rum to them and would only sell small quantities of powder and shot. Things under the English were looking worse. Similar disturbing experiences were the lot of Native peoples trading at several interior posts. During the next year, Native delegates travelled from village to village carrying the rumour that the French king would send an army with supplies and ammunition up the Mississippi to help the Natives drive out the English. By 1763, the insults, the rumours and the prophecies boiled into open warfare against the English.

When the uprising finally broke out in the spring, the Ottawa, Chippewa, Wyandot and Pottawatomie, with allies from other nations, successfully captured Michilimackinac and laid siege to Detroit. Pontiac attempted to take the fort by stealth on May 7, 1763, but was countered by the alertness of post commander Major Henry Gladwyn. Pontiac then kept Detroit isolated and, under siege until the autumn of 1763, when he had to give up on the plan to capture it.

Small Seneca war parties, usually from villages along the Genesee River (the so-called Chenussio Seneca) and from the westernmost Seneca homelands, had been out on campaign since the spring. They assisted Chippewa warriors with the capture of forts Presqu'ile, Venango and Le Boeuf, and by the end of the summer they controlled all of the land between Lake Ontario and the forks of the Ohio. Fort Pitt was besieged but could not be captured. The Native force attacking that post suffered heavily in a battle known as Bushy Run. At Niagara, the main action of this 1763 warfare occurred on the portage route between Fort Niagara and Lewiston Heights at a place opposite the Niagara River whirlpool rapids known as "Devil's Glen," which the Seneca believed was haunted by malevolent spirits. It was here, on September 14, that they ambushed a supply train from Fort Niagara, killing 72 English and capturing supplies in a lightning-quick strike.

The summer's campaign had exhausted the supply of gunpowder available to the warriors and what little they had left had to be saved for the crucial autumn hunt. With the English posts at Detroit, Niagara and Pittsburgh still holding into the autumn, most warriors realized that they could not win this war. They also realized that French help would not be forthcoming.

William Johnson and Six Nations leaders continually worked to try to bring peace through diplomacy. Many elders in the various Nations similarly tried to bring the more hot-headed young warriors to an understanding of the futility in continuing the war. By the autumn, things had become quiet on the frontier.

When the spring arrived, Native leaders learned that the English had made the Proclamation of 1763, barring further white encroachment west of the Allegheny Mountains. Amherst was recalled and Johnson's diplomatic efforts were paying off. While small parties of warriors continued to be active, the war was effectively over.

There was some reason for optimism following the risings. The English authorities recognized the importance of gifts, the need to prevent further encroachments on Native lands and the fact that Native people had to be treated with respect and dignity. These concessions gave Native peoples a false sense of hope that their sovereignty would be preserved. However, the proclamation line would be redrawn and redrawn over the next generation, continually pushing the boundary for white settlement west.

While the Proclamation of 1763 gave the Native peoples of the Ohio Valley–Great Lakes basins some hope, it infuriated many in the American colonies who felt hemmed in by the new boundary and angry that the English had treated the Natives too leniently. The groundwork of another rebellion was being laid.

The Seeds of Revolt

During the war with France, the American colonies had evolved from a fractious group of English colonies into a unit that by war's end was acting in concert to provide material assistance to the English war effort. In many ways, the bumbling General Abercromby can be credited with developing a coordinated system of recruitment, supply and transportation in the colonies. The Albany congress of 1754 had attempted to achieve this coordination but had failed because some of the delegates, including Benjamin Franklin, wanted the colonies to become much more cohesive. Many of the delegates and most of the colonial governors were reluctant to form any sort of unified government at that time. However, some of the arguments for working closely together now made more sense after several years of hostilities.

The war had also built an incredible spirit of pride in the military abilities of the colonists. Americans had formed effective ranger units, had built fleets of batteaux, cut roads through vast expanses of wilderness, constructed strong forts and fought, and won, campaigns against the professional soldiers of France and their Native allies. They had also seen English regulars defeated at places like forts Duquesne and Carillon. In addition, many Americans had developed a dislike of the English as a result of the haughty attitudes of many regular officers in their dealings with the colonial soldiers.

Many Americans believed that the defeat of the French opened the way for westward expansion into the interior of the continent. Immediate exploitation was delayed by the various small wars with Native nations in 1763, but the hope was that the way would finally be cleared for land speculators and homesteaders. The Proclamation of 1763, reinforced by the Treaty of Fort Stanwix five years later, prevented the westward move and this upset many Americans who felt they had earned the right to take this land through their sacrifices during the war.

Finally, the English parliament decided to levy heavy taxes on the Americans to recover the costs of the Seven Years War. Among other acts, the Stamp Act particularly focused American attention on the fact that the parliament of England was levying taxes on them without permitting direct American representation in the English parliament. Eventually, the discontent gained momentum and, by 1775, had evolved into armed rebellion that would only end with the granting of American independence in 1783.

The Legacy of War

The Seven Years War in America is not well known. In the United States it has been overshadowed by the history of the American Revolution and of the Civil War 90 years later. Canadians tend to think of the war only in terms of one of its battles — the Plains of Abraham. Two of its principal players, Wolfe and Montcalm, tend to be known and many Canadians have a vague idea that at one point Acadians were exiled from their land. For many French Canadians the war represents the beginning of their country's occupation by a foreign power. "Je me souviens," a prominent slogan in Quebec, shows that the Quebecois remember the days before the conquest.

The Seven Years War had a major impact on the people of North America. The bicultural and bilingual nature of Canada had its roots in the terms of the Capitulation of Montreal, which permitted the Canadiens to retain their religion, language and civil law. The roles played by colonists from the English colonies and the removal of the French army and its control of the Ohio Valley influenced events that led to the American Revolution and the establishment of the United States of America. That, in turn, led to tens of thousands of refugees leaving the new republic to continue to live under the British crown. These Loyalists established many communities in Atlantic Canada and laid the foundations for Ontario.

A re-enactment of the English attack on Fort Niagara. The French withdrawal from North America had a huge impact on the future of the continent.

Finally, the war had a major impact on the fate of many Native nations. The conflict changed course from 1754, when Native alliances were crucial to victory, to 1760, when the war was fought by trained armies using European-style tactics and Natives took on a peripheral role. During the war a gap had been driven between the white people of the frontier and the Natives who occupied the land they coveted. This was to have a major effect on the ways in which the whites would deal with Native people in the future, to the detriment of the First Nations of America. Although the various nations had not capitulated or ceded their lands, and had not lost any major battles, at the end of the war it was considered that the English now "owned," or at least controlled, the land east of the Mississippi River and west of the Great Lakes. The sovereignty of Native nations was badly undermined by the French and Indian War.

Few wars end without having an impact on future events, and this war had many. Native peoples in eastern North America still struggle with the legal consequences of treaties signed and implied in the transfer of power from the French to the English. Canadiens still struggle to assert their rights and maintain their distinct culture. The descendents of the displaced Acadians research to puzzle together the story of their ancestors and visit the sites from which they were expelled. At the Fortress of Louisbourg, the Fortifications of Quebec, Fort Anne in Annapolis Royal, Fort Niagara, Fort Necessity, Oswego and Ticonderoga, and many other battlefields of the war, the spirits of these places still speak and the drama of these great events remains a tangible presence.

HISTORICAL DOCUMENTS

There are many letters, journals and other eyewitness accounts of the French and Indian War. The following represents a sampling of what can be gleaned from these documents.

Cornwallis' speech to the Acadian Delegates, July 28, 1755

We have cause to be much astonished at your conduct. This is the third time that you have come here from your departments, and you do nothing but repeat the same story without the least change. To-day you present us a letter signed by a thousand persons, in which you declare openly that you will be the subjects of His Britannic Majesty, only on such and such conditions. It appears to me that you think yourselves independent of any government; and you wish to treat with the King as if you were so.

Gentlemen, you allow yourselves to be led away by people who find it to their interest to lead you astray. They have made you imagine it is only your oath which binds you to the English. They deceive you. It is not the oath which a King administers to his subjects that makes them subjects. The oath supposes that they are so already. The oath is nothing but a very sacred bond of the fidelity of those who take it. It is only out of pity to your situations, and to your inexperience in the affairs of government, that we condescend to reason with you; otherwise, Gentlemen, the question would not be reasoning, but commanding and being obeyed.

Letter on the Deportation of the Acadians sent to Colonel Monckton, July 31, 1755

In the mean time, it will be necessary to keep this measure as secret as possible, as well to prevent their attempting to escape, as to carry off their cattle &c.; and the better to effect this you will endeavour to fall upon some stratagem to get the men, both young and old (especially the heads of families) into your power and detain them till the transports shall arrive, so as that they may be ready to be shipped off; for when this is done it is not much to be feared that the women and children will attempt to go away and carry off the cattle. But least they should, it will not only be very proper to secure all their Shallops, Boats, Canoes and every other vessel you can lay your hands upon; But also to send out parties to all suspected roads and places from time to time, that they may be thereby intercepted. As their whole stock of Cattle and Corn is forfeited to the Crown by their rebellion, and must be secured & apply'd towards a reimbursement of the expense the government will be at in transporting them out of the Country, care must be had that nobody make any bargain for purchasing them under any colour or pretence whatever; if they do the sale will be void, for the inhabitants have now (since the order in Council) no property in them, nor will they be allowed to carry away the least thing but their ready money and household furniture.

The officers commanding the Fort at Piziquid and the Garrison of Annapolis Royal have nearly the same orders in relation to the interior Inhabitants.

George Washington to his mother concerning Braddock's Defeat

HONORED MADAM: As I doubt not but you have heard of our defeat, and, perhaps, had it represented in a worse light, if possible, than it deserves, I have taken this earliest opportunity to give you some account of the engagement as it happened, within ten miles of the French fort, on Wednesday the 9th instant.

We marched to that place, without any considerable loss, having only now and then a straggler picked up by the French and scouting Indians. When we came there, we were attacked by a party of French and Indians, whose number, I am persuaded, did not exceed three hundred men; while ours consisted of about one thousand three hundred well-armed troops, chiefly regular soldiers, who were struck with such a panic that they behaved with more cowardice than it is possible to conceive. The officers behaved gallantly, in order to encourage their men, for which they suffered greatly, there being near sixty killed and wounded; a large proportion of the number we had.

The Virginia troops showed a good deal of bravery, and were nearly all killed; for I believe, out of three companies that were there, scarcely thirty men are left alive. Captain Peyrouny, and all his officers down to a corporal, were killed. Captain Polson had nearly as hard a fate, for only one of his was left. In short, the dastardly behavior of those they call regulars exposed all others, that were inclined to do their duty, to almost certain death; and, at last, in despite of all the efforts of the officers to the contrary, they ran, as sheep pursued by dogs, and it was impossible to rally them.

French Account of Braddock's Defeat

M. De Contrecoeur, Captain of Infantry, Commandant of Fort Duquesne, on the Ohio, having been informed that the English were taking up arms in Virginia for the purpose of coming to attack him, was advised, shortly afterwards, that they were on the march. He dispatched scouts, who reported to him faithfully their progress. On the 17th instant he was advised that their army, consisting of 3000 regulars from Old England, were within six leagues of this fort. That officer employed the next day in making his arrangements; and on the ninth detached M. de Beaujeu, seconded by Messrs Dumas and de Lignery, all three Captains, together with four Lieutenants, 6 Ensigns, 20 Cadets, 100 Soldiers, 100 Canadians and 600 Indians, with orders to lie in ambush at a favorable spot, which he had reconnoitred the previous evening. The detachment, before it could reach its place of

destination, found itself in presence of the enemy within three leagues of that fort. M. de Beaujeu, finding his ambush had failed, decided on an attack. This he made with so much vigor as to astonish the enemy, who were waiting for us in the best possible order; but their artillery, loaded with grape shot, having opened its fire, our men gave way in turn. The Indians, also, frightened by the report of the cannon rather than by any damage it could inflict, began to yield, when M. de Beaujeu was killed. M. Dumas began to encourage his detachment. He ordered the officers in command of the Indians to spread themselves along the wings so as to take the enemy in flank, whilst he, M. de Lignery and the other officers who led the French, were attacking them in front. This order was executed so promptly that the enemy, who were already shouting their "Long live the King," thought now only of defending themselves. The fight was obstinate on both sides and success long doubtful; but the enemy at last gave way. Efforts were made, in vain, to introduce some sort of order in their retreat. The whoop of the Indians, which echoed through the forest, struck terror into the hearts of the entire enemy. The rout was complete. We remained in possession of the field with six brass twelves and sixes, four five inch howitzers, 11 small royal grenade mortars, all their ammunition, and, generally, their entire baggage. Some deserters, who have come in since, have told us that we had been engaged with only 2000 men, the remainder of the army being four leagues further off. These same deserters have informed us that the enemy were retreating to Virginia, and some scouts, sent as far as the height of land, have confirmed this by reporting that the thousand men who were not engaged, had been equally panic-stricken and abandoned both provisions and ammunition on the way. On this intelligence, a detachment was dispatched after them, which destroyed and burnt everything that could be found. The enemy have left more than 1000 men on the field of battle. They have lost a great portion of the artillery and ammunition, provisions, as also their General, whose name was Mr Braddock, and almost all their officers. We have had 3 officers killed; 2 officers and 2 cadets wounded. Such a victory, so entirely unexpected, seeing the inequality of the forces, is the fruit of Mr Dumas' experience, and of the activity and valor of the officers under his command.

Battle of Lake George described in a letter from Baron de Dieskau to Count d'Argenson

14th September, 1755

On the very vague intelligence of the designs of the English in that quarter, I proceeded thither with 3000 men, whereof 700 were Regulars, 1600 Canadians, and 700 Indians. I arrived at Fort St. Frederic on the 16th and 17th of August; a portion of the troops had proceeded me; the remainder joined me there without delay. Before quitting Montreal, I had already various reasons for suspecting the fidelity of the domiciliated Iroquois, both of the Sault St. Louis and that of the Lake of the Two Mountains, whose number exceeded 300, composing half of the Indians that had been given to me. I represented it repeatedly to M. de Vaudreuil, who would never admit it, but scarcely had I arrived at Fort St. Frederic, than I had occasion to furnish him still stronger proofs thereof.

At length, on the 27th of August, a Canadian named Boileau, returned from a scout and informed me that about 3000 English were encamped at Lidius' house, where they were constructing a fort that was already pretty well advanced. I immediately resolved to go forward and to post myself in an advantageous place, either to wait for the enemy, should he advance, or to anticipate him myself, by going in quest of him. On arriving at this post, some Abenakis who had been on the scout, unknown to the Iroquois, brought me in an English prisoner, who told me that the body of the English army had moved from Lidius', and that only 500 remained there to finish the fort, but that they were expecting 2400 men, who were to march to the head of Lake St. Sacrament for the purpose of Building a fort there also.

On this intelligence I determined to leave the main body of the army where I was, and to take with me a picked force and march rapidly and surprise Fort Lidius, and capture the 500 men encamped without its walls. My detachement was composed of 600 Indians, 600 Canadians and 200 Regulars belonging to La Reine and Languedoc Regiments. It was four days' journey by water and across the woods to Lidius. All exhibited an ardor which guaranteed success, but the fourth day, which ought to be favorable to the King's arms, was the commencement of our misfortune. The Iroquois refused point blank to march to attack the fort, or rather the camp of the 500 English; but, perceiving that I was resolved to dispence with them, and that the other Indians were disposed to follow me, they sent excuses and immediately set forth to lead the van, as if to make a parade of their zeal.

A courier that was killed, and whose despatch was brought to me, and some prisoners that were brought in, gave me the intelligence that about 3000 English were encamped near there, and that they had but a confused knowledge of the strength of my forces. I immediately gave the Indians the choice of proceeding next day to attack either the fort or this army. The vote of the Iroquois, which prevailed, caused the latter course to be adopted. On the following day, the 8th of September, I commenced my march. About 10 of the clock, after having proceeded 5 leagues, the scouts reported to me that they had seen a large body of troops on their way to the fort, which news was confirmed by a prisoner, taken at the time. They consisted of one thousand men or more, that had left the camp to reinforce the fort. I immediately made my arrangements, ordered the Indians to throw themselves into the woods, to allow the enemy to pass, so as to attack them in the rear, whilst the Canadians took them on the flank, and I should wait for them in front with the regular troops.

As I was near the enemy's camp, and in front of the cannon, I marched forward with 200 Regulars to capture it, expecting that the Canadians would not abandon me, and that the Indians would perhaps return; but in vain. The Regulars received the whole of the enemy's fire and perished there almost to a man. I was knocked down by three shots, none of which were mortal, but I received a 4th that passed from one hip to the other, perforating the bladder.

The Capture of Quebec described by General Townshend, 20 September, 1759

It being determined to carry the Operations above the town, the Posts at Point Levi & L'Isle d'Orleans being secured the General march'd with the remainder of his Force from Point Levi the 5th & 6th & embarked them in Transports which had passed the Town for that Purpose; on the 7th 8th & 9th a movement of the Ships was made up by Admiral Holmes in order to amuse the Enemy now posted along the North Shore, but the Transports being extreamly crowded and the weather very bad the General thought proper to canton half his Troops on the South Shore, where they were refresh'd and reimbark'd upon the 12th at one in the morning. The Light Infantry commanded by Colonel Howe The Regiments of Braggs, Kennedys, Lascelles & Anstruthers, with a Detachment of Highlanders and the American Grenadiers. The whole being under the Command of Brigadiers Monckton & Murray were put into the Flat Bottom'd Boats & after some Movement of the Ships made by Admiral Holmes to draw the attention of the Enemy above, The Boats fell down with the Tide & Landed on the North Shore within a League of Cape Diamond an Hour before Day Break. The rapidity of the Tide of Ebb carried them a little below the intended place of attack — which obliged the Light Infantry to Scramble up a woody precipice in order to secure the landing the troops by dislodging a Captains Post which defended the small intrench'd Path the Troops were to ascend — after a little Firing the Light Infantry gained the top of the Precipice, & dispersed the Captains Post by which means the Troops with very little loss from a few Canadians & Indians in the Wood got up & were immediately form'd. The Boats as they emptied, were sent back for the 2nd Disembarkation which I immediately made Brigr. Murray being detached with Anstruther's Battalion to attack the 4 Gun Battery upon the left, was recall'd by the General who now saw the French Army crossing the River St. Charles. General Wolfe thereupon began to form his Line having his right covered by the Louisbourg Grenadiers — on the right of these again he afterwards brought Otways — to the left of the Grenadiers were Braggs, Kennedys, Lascelles, Highlanders & Anstruther's. The right of this body was comanded by Brigr. Monckton & the left by Brigr. Murray his rear & left was protected by Col. Howe's Light Infantry, who was return'd from the 4 gun Battery before mention'd, which was soon abandon'd to him, where he found 4 Guns of General Montcalm having collected the whole of his Force from the Beauport side, & advancing upon shew'd his Intention to flank our left, where I was immediately ordered with Genl. Amhersts' Battalion which I form'd en potence, my numbers were soon after encreased by the Arrival of the 2 Battalions of Royal Americans, and Webbs was drawn up by the General as a Reserve in Eight Subdivisions with large Intervals. The

Enemy lined the Bushes in their Front with 1500 Indians & Canadians & I dare say had placed most of their best Marksmen there, who kept up a very galling tho' irregular fire upon our whole Line, who bore it with the greatest patience and good Order; reserving their fire for the Main body now advancing. This fire of the Enemies was however check'd by our posts in our front, which protected the forming our own Line.

The right of the Enemy was composed of half of the Troops of the Colony, the Battns, of La Sarre, Languedoc, & the remainder of their Canadians & Indians. Their Center was a Column & form'd by the Battalions of Bearn & Guyenne. Their left was composed of the remainder of the Troops of the Colony and the Battalion of Royal Rousillion. This was as near as I guess their Line of Battle. They brought up 2 pieces of small Artillery against us and we had been able to bring up but one Gun, which being admirably well served gall'd their Column exceedingly. My attention to the left will not permit me to be very exact with regard to every Circumstance which passed in the Center, much less to the right, but it is most certain that the Enemy form'd in good Order, & that their attack was very brisk & animated on that side, our Troops reserved their Fire till within 20 Yards which was so well continued that the Enemy everywhere gave way. T'was there our General fell at the Head of Braggs & the Louisbourg Grenadiers, advancing with their Bayonets, about the same time B. General Monkton received his wound at the head of Lascelles; In the front of the opposite Battalions fell also Monr. Montcalm, & his Second in Command since died of his wounds on board our fleet. Part of the Enemy made a second feint attack, part took to some thick copse Wood & seem'd to make a Stand. It was at this Moment that each Corps seemd in a manner to exert itself with a view to its own peculiar Character, the Grenadiers, Braggs & Lascelles press'd on with their Bayonets. Brigadier Murray advancing the Troops under his Command brisky compleated the Route on this side when the Highlanders supported by Anstruthers took to their Broad Swords & drove part into the Town, part to the works at their Bridge on the River St. Charles.

Recommended Reading

Published Histories

Many histories have been written about the Seven Years War and its battles over the past two centuries. The following represent a sampling of books that are extensively researched and very well written:

Anderson, Fred. *A People's Army: Massachusetts Soldiers and Society in the Seven Years' War*. University of North Carolina, Chapel Hill, 1984.

Anderson, Fred. *Crucible of War: The Seven Years' War and the Fate of Empire in British North America, 1754-1766*. Random House, New York, 2001.

Chartrand, Rene. *Quebec 1759: The Heights of Abraham; the Armies of Wolfe and Montcalm*. Osprey, London, 1999.

Chartrand, Rene. *Canadian Military Heritage, Vol. 1: 1000-1754*. Art Global, Montreal, 1993.

Chartrand, Rene. *Canadian Military Heritage, Vol. 2: 1755-1871*. Art Global, Montreal, 1995.

Dunnigan, Brian Leigh. *Siege 1759: The Campaign Against Niagara*. Old Fort Niagara Association, Youngstown, 1986.

MacLeod, D. Peter. *The Canadian Iroquois and the Seven Years' War*. Dundurn Press, Toronto, 1996.

Stacey, C.P. *Quebec 1759: The Siege and the Battle*. Revised edition edited by Donald E. Graves, Robin Brass, Toronto, 2002.

Original Accounts

There have been a great number of eyewitness accounts written about the Seven Years War in North America, but the following are especially colourful:

Bougainville, Louis-Antoine de. *Écrits sur le Canada: mémoires, journal, lettres*. republished by Pelican, Paris, 1993.

Knox, John. *An Historical Journal of the Campaigns in North America for the Years 1757, 1758, 1759 and 1760*. Originally published in 1769; edited by Arthur G. Doughty and republished by the Champlain Society, Toronto, 1915.

Pouchot, Pierre. *Memoirs of the Late War in North America between France and England*. Originally printed in 1781; translated by Michael Cardy and edited and annotated by Brian Dunnigan in 1994; republished by the Old Fort Niagara Association, Youngstown, 1994.

Seaver, James. *A Narrative of the life of Mrs. Mary Jemison*. Originally published in 1824; republished by Syracuse University, Syracuse, 1990.

ASSOCIATED SITES

A number of historic sites at which the events of this book took place have been carefully preserved through the efforts of both government and private citizens in Canada and the United States. These special places offer fascinating interpretive programs that help the visitor to gain a deeper understanding of the significant stories that unfolded at these forts and battlefields. The following historic sites are recommended:

Canada

Fort Anne National Historic Site of Canada

P.O. Box 9, Annapolis Royal, Nova Scotia, B0S 1A0
phone: (902) 532-2397
www.pc.ca/lhn-nhs/ns/fortanne
Fort Anne, in Annapolis Royal, Nova Scotia, is Canada's first National Historic Site. The original fortifications of the French and English forts, including the original French powder magazine, are preserved at this site overlooking the shores of the Annapolis River.

Fort Edward National Historic Site of Canada

P.O. Box 9, Annapolis Royal, Nova Scotia, B0S 1A0
phone: (902) 532-2321
www.pc.gc.ca/lhn-nhs/ns/edward
Not far from Fort Anne is Fort Edward in West Hants, Nova Scotia. The site preserves the oldest blockhouse in Canada and remnants of the original earthworks of this English post.

Grand Pré National Historic Site of Canada

P.O. Box 150, Grand Pré, Nova Scotia, B0P 1M0
phone: (902) 542-3631
www.pc.gc.ca/lhn-nhs/ns/grandpre
Grand Pré in Nova Scotia is a 14-acre site featuring gardens, monuments and statues commemorating the Acadian village here and the deportation of the Acadians in 1755.

Halifax Citadel National Historic Site of Canada

P.O. Box 9080, Station A, Halifax, Nova Scotia, B3K 5M7
phone: (902) 426-5080
www.pc.gc.ca/lhn-nhs/ns/halifax
The citadel is a 19th century fort on the site of earlier fortifications built by the English before the Seven Years War. Exhibits trace the site's early history while period demonstrations give visitors a vivid idea of life at the fort in the latter half of the 19th century.

Fortress of Louisbourg National Historic Site of Canada

259 Park Service Road, Louisbourg, Nova Scotia, B1C 2L2
phone: (902) 733-2280
www.pc.gc.ca/lhn-nhs/ns/louisbourg
The fortress of Louisbourg is a large-scale reconstruction of the town and fortress of Louisbourg, located on Cape Breton Island in Nova Scotia. The site features many restored stone buildings interpreted by staff dressed in authentic period costume. During the summer, the site comes alive with military drills and demonstrations of civilian life.

Fort Beauséjour National Historic Site of Canada

111 Fort Beauséjour Road, Aulac, New Brunswick , E4L 2W5
phone: (506) 364-5080
www.pc.gc.ca/lhn-nhs/nb/beausejour
Fort Beauséjour in Aulac, New Brunswick, near the Nova Scotia border preserves the ruins of the fort that challenged English sovereignty in Nova Scotia. Earthworks and the excavated foundations of the original fort buildings overlook a beautiful natural landscape.

Battle of the Restigouche National Historic Site of Canada

P.O. Box 359, Route 132, Pointe-à-la-Croix, Quebec, G0C 1L0
phone: 1-800-463-6769
www.pc.gc.ca/lhn-nhs/qc/restigouche
This site, at the mouth of the Restigouche River near Pointe-á-la-Croix, Quebec, is the site of the sinking of the French frigate *Machault*. The ship has been explored by Parks Canada underwater archaeologists and many of its artifacts are on display at the interpretation centre located here.

Quebec

2 D'Auteuil Street, P.O.Box 2474, Postal Terminal, Quebec, QC, G1K 7R3
phone: (418) 648-4205
www.pc.gc.ca/lhn-nhs/qc/artillery

The city of Quebec preserves a number of National Historic Sites associated with the war. The Plains of Abraham, the Fortifications of Quebec, Artillery Park and others are surrounded by original buildings that stood at the time of Wolfe's bombardment of the city. Streets familiar to Montcalm and Vaudreuil appear much as they would have in 1759.

Fort Chambly National Historic Site of Canada

2 De Richelieu Street, Chambly, Quebec, J3L 2B9
phone: (450) 658-1585
www.pc.gc.ca/lhn-nhs/qc/fortchambly

Fort Lennox National Historic Site of Canada

1 61st Avenue, Saint-Paul-de-l'Île-aux-Noix, Quebec, J0J 1G0
phone: (450) 291-5700
www.pc.gc.ca/lhn-nhs/qc/lennox

Fort Chambly, on the Richelieu River at Chambly, Quebec, preserves the important French fort built in 1711 to guard the invasion route from Lake Champlain. Its imposing stone walls house interpretive exhibits that explore the history of the site. Nearby Fort Lennox on Île-aux-Noix in the Richelieu River is a beautifully preserved early 19th century English fort built near the French fort and dockyard of the French and Indian War period.

United States

Fort Necessity National Battlefield

One Washington Parkway, Farmington, PA, 15437
phone: (724) 329-5805
www.nps.gov/fone

Fort Necessity is a 900-acre park in southwestern Pennsylvania that preserves the sites of Washington's Fort Necessity, the Braddock grave and Jumonville Glen. The palisade of the fort has been reconstructed and interpretive programs guide the visitor to the history of the sites.

Fort Pitt Museum

101 Commonwealth Place, Point State Park, Pittsburgh, Pennsylvania, 15222
phone: (412) 281-9284
www.fortpittmuseum.com

While Fort Duquesne and Fort Pitt were buried by urban development in Pittsburgh, this museum near the location of the forts preserves the stories and archaeological artifacts related to this important site at the forks of the Ohio.

Fort Ticonderoga

PO Box 390, Ticonderoga, N.Y., 12883
phone: (518) 585-2821
www.fort-ticonderoga.org

Fort Ticonderoga in New York State preserves the English fort built on the ruins of the earlier French fortification. While the focus of the fort is on the Revolutionary War period, this fort, along with the historic site at nearby Crown Point, give the visitor a good idea of the terrain and strategic importance of these locations when they were the sites of French forts Carillon and Sainte-Frédéric.

Fort Ontario State Historic Site

1 East Fourth Street, Oswego, NY, 13126
phone: (315) 343-4711; Fax: (315) 343-1430
www.nysparks.state.ny

While Fort Ontario in Oswego, New York, is restored to its late 1860's appearance and its buildings and fortifications are restored 19th century American constructions, the site preserves the earlier history of the three forts at the mouth of the Oswego river that were the scene of siege and massacre.

Fort Michilimackinac State Historic Park

P.O. Box 873, Mackinaw City, MI, 49701
phone: 231-436-4100; Fax: 231-436-4210
www.mackinacparks.com/michilimackinac

Fort Michilimackinac, constructed by the French in 1715 and destroyed during the Native uprising of 1763, has been carefully archaeologically excavated and reconstructed. The log buildings are brought to life each summer by staff in period costume.

Old Fort Niagara National Historic Landmark

P.O. Box 169, Youngstown, NY, 14174-0169
phone: (716) 745-7611
www.oldfortniagara.org

Fort Niagara, constructed by the French in 1726 and scene of so much activity in the Seven Years War, the 1763 Native uprising, the American Revolution and the War of 1812, is the best preserved original fort that was active during the Seven Years War. The original French powder magazine, massive "castle" and bakehouse along with post-conquest English buildings make this a "must visit" site. An ongoing archaeological project has unearthed many reminders of the English siege of the fort in 1759.

INDEX

f. 9/2015 S

Visual credits:

Legend: Top – T; Center – C;
Bottom – B; Left – L; Right – R
NAC – National Archives of Canada

Maps by Peggy McCalla

60th Regiment of Foot (Royal
Americans), by Barry Rich, © Parks
Canada, 19

Abenakis Indians, © Parks Canada, 26

Acadian Militia, by Derek Fitzjames,
© Parks Canada, 27B

Algonquin Indians, © Parks Canada,
24TL

Angel Art Photography, 15, 21B,
50BR, 56, 85

Bearn Regiment, by Eugéne Leliépvre,
© Parks Canada, 23

Beveridge, Julian, 33

Bowles, Carrington/NAC/C-001090, 12

Bray, George, 55B, 64T

Brompton, Richard/NAC/C-121919,
55T

Campion, George B./NAC/ C-004501,
64B

Canadian militiamen, by Francis Back,
© Parks Canada, 70

Canadian Museum of Civilization, 9B,
18R, 29B, 30B, 36T, 40TR, 42B,
44T, 50BL, 80, 82

Carpenter, Phil, 59T, 71

Davies, Thomas/NAC/C-010653, 50T

Derby Museum and Art Gallery, 57

de Champlain, Samuel/National
Library of Canada, 8T

Desbarres, Joseph Frederick
Wallet/NAC/C-002705, 29T

Drummer, Compagnies Franches de la
Marine, by Michel Pétard, © Parks
Canada, 8B

Fort Ontario State Historical Site, 14,
35T

Glens Falls Insurance Company, 43, 49

Granger Collection, 4E233.12, 81

Grasset de Saint-Sauveur,
Jacques/NAC/C-003163, 16

Hamilton, John/NAC/C-002706, 20B

Hamilton, John/NAC/C-002707, 28B

Jefferys, Charles William/NAC/
C-073700, 79

Jefferys, Charles William/NAC/
C-073720, 63

Jefferys, Charles William/NAC/
C-069336, 30T

Jefferys, Charles William/NAC/
C-069902, 31T

Jefferys, Charles William/NAC/
C-070232, 32T

Jefferys, Charles William/NAC/
C-073709, 31B

La Reine and Languedoc Regiments,
Eugéne Leliépvre, © Parks Canada,
47T

Lagliore, Theodore, 60T

Massachusetts Militia (WM. Shirley's
Regiment), by Derek Fitzjames,
© Parks Canada, 18L

Micmac Indian, by Derek Fitzjames,
© Parks Canada, 28T

Micmac Warrior, by Francis Back,
© Parks Canada, 32B

Munroe, Norman, 46T

NAC/C-000799, 35B

NAC/C-001078, 58B

NAC/C-001457, 75T

NAC/C-002069, 72

NAC/C-002834, 67

NAC/C-006017, 51

NAC/C-007700, 41T

NAC/C-009418, 34B

NAC/C-024549, 27T

NAC/C-034786, 83

NAC/C-040575, 11

NAC/C-041003, 66

NAC/C-062181, 74T

NAC/C-062197, 36B

NAC/C-083497, 20T

NAC/C-099253, 9T

NAC/C-112058, 74B

NAC/C-147536, 40TL

National Gallery of Canada/8004, 44B

Nova Scotia Historical Society, 13

Officer, Roger's Rangers, by Barry Rich,
© Parks Canada, 42T

Officer, Royal Engineers, by Barry
Rich, © Parks Canada, 69B

Parks Canada, 10, 22T, 46B, 75B

Paton, Richard/NAC/C-143388, 47B

Poulin, Stephane, 60B

Pyle, Howard/NAC/C-007220, 25T

Récollet priest, by Francis Back,
© Parks Canada, 69T

Rudyerd, Henry/NAC/C-040336, 39

Sargent, Antoine Louis
François/NAC/C-014342, 34T

Schuessele, C./NAC/C-002644, 24B

Scotin, I.B./NAC/C-001854, 7

Scott, Adam Sherriff/NAC/ C-011043,
77

Serres, Dominic/NAC/C-004291, 58T

Short, Richard/NAC/C-000350, 68

Short, Richard/NAC/C-000352, 59B

Short, Richard/NAC/C-000357, 61

Short, Richard/NAC/C-041433, 78

Short, Richard/NAC/C-000351, 1

Short, Richard/NAC/C-000355, 53

Smyth Swaine, Hervey Frances/NAC/
C-000788, 62

Soldier, Compagnies Franches de la
Marine, by Derek Fitzjames, © Parks
Canada, 54

Soldier, Compagnies Franches de la
Marine, by Francis Back, © Parks
Canada, 40

Stewart Museum, Montreal, 21T, 22B,
24TR, 41B

Toronto Reference Library Picture
Collection, 17T, 17B, 52

Townsend, George/ Reilly, Robin. *The
Rest to Fortune, The Life and Times of
Major-General James Wolfe*. London:
Cassell & Company Ltd. 1960, 45

Verelst, John/NAC/C-092418, 25B

Verelst, John/NAC/C-092420, 37

West, Benjamin/National Gallery of
Canada, 65